Kate Seymour MacLean

The Coming of the Princess

And Other Poems

Kate Seymour MacLean

The Coming of the Princess
And Other Poems

ISBN/EAN: 9783744714150

Printed in Europe, USA, Canada, Australia, Japan

Cover: Foto ©Thomas Meinert / pixelio.de

More available books at **www.hansebooks.com**

THE COMING OF THE PRINCESS;

AND

OTHER POEMS.

BY

KATE SEYMOUR MACLEAN,
KINGSTON, ONTARIO.

AN INTRODUCTION,

BY THE EDITOR OF "THE CANADIAN MONTHLY."

Toronto:
HUNTER, ROSE & COMPANY.
MDCCCLXXXI.

Entered according to Act of Parliament of Canada, in the year one thousand eight hundred and eighty-one, by HUNTER ROSE & Co., in the office of the Minister of Agriculture.

INTRODUCTION.

BY G. MERCER ADAM.

THE request of the author that I should write a few words of preface to this collection of poems must be my excuse for obtruding myself upon the reader. Having frequently had the pleasure, as editor of *The Canadian Monthly*, of introducing many of Mrs. MacLean's poems to lovers of verse in the Dominion, it was thought not unfitting that I should act as foster-father to the collection of them here made, and to bespeak for the volume, at the hands at least of all Canadians, the appreciative and kindly reception due to a

"Child of the first winds and suns of a nation."

Accepting the task assigned to me, the more readily as I discern the high and sustained excellence of the collection as a whole, let me ask that the volume be received with interest, as a further and most meritorious contribution to the poetical literature of our young country (the least that can be said of the work), and with sympathy for the intellectual and moral aspirations that have called it into being.

There is truth, doubtless, in the remark, that we are enriched less by what we have than by what we hope to have. As the poetic art in Canada has had little of an appreciable past, it may therefore be thought that the songs that are to catch and retain the ear of the nation lie still in the future, and are as yet unsung. Doubtless the chords have yet to be struck that are to give to Canada the songs of her loftiest genius; but he would be an ill friend of the country's literature who would slight the achievements of the present in reaching solely after what, it is hoped, the coming time will bring.

But whatever of lyrical treasure the future may enshrine in Canadian literature, and however deserving may be the claims of the volumes of verse that have already appeared from the native press, I am bold to claim for these productions of Mrs. MacLean's muse a high place in the national collection and a warm corner in the national heart.

To discern the merit of a poem is proverbially easier than to say how and in what manner it is manifested. In a collection the task of appraisement is not so difficult. Lord Houghton has said: "There is in truth no critic of poetry but the man who enjoys it, and the amount of gratification felt is the only just measure of criticism." By this test the present volume will, in the main, be judged. Still, there are characteristics of the author's work which I may be permitted to point out. In Mrs. MacLean's volume what quickly strikes one is not only the fact that the poems are all of a high order of merit, but that a large measure of art and instinct enters into the composition of each of them. As readily will it be recognized that they are the product of a cultivated intellect, a bright fancy, and a feeling heart. A rich spiritual life breathes throughout the work, and there are occasional manifestations of fervid impulse and ardent feeling. Yet there is no straining of expression in the poems, nor is there any loose fluency of thought. Throughout there is sustained elevation and lofty purpose. Her least work, moreover, is worthy of her, because it is always honest work. With a quiet simplicity of style, there is at the same time a fine command of language and an earnest beauty of thought. The grace and melody of the versification, indeed, few readers will fail to appreciate. Occasionally there are echoes of other poets—Jean Ingelow and Mrs. Barrett Browning, in the more subjective pieces, being oftenest suggested. But there is a voice as well as an echo—the voice of a poet in her own right. In an age so bustling and heedless as this, it were well sometimes to stop and listen to the voice. In its fine spiritualizations we shall at least be soothed and may be bettered.

But I need not dwell on the vocation of poetry or on the excellence of the poems here introduced. The one is well known to the reader: the other may soon be. Happily there is promise that Canada will ere long be rich in her poets. They stand in the vanguard of a country's benefactors, and so should be cherished and encouraged. Of late our serial literature has given us more than blossomings. The present volume enshrines some of the maturer fruit. May it be its mission to nourish the poetic sentiment among us. May it do more! —nourish in some degree the heart of the nation, and, in the range of its influence, that of humanity

CANADIAN MONTHLY OFFICE,
    Toronto, December, 1880.

CONTENTS.

	PAGE.
INTRODUCTION	iii
ENVOI	xi
The Coming of the Princess	1
Bird Song	7
An Idyl of the May	9
The Burial of the Scout	14
Questionings	16
Pansies	19
November Meteors	22
Pictures in the Fire	26
A Madrigal	28
The Ploughboy	30
The Voice of Many Waters	32
The Death of Autumn	34
A Farewell	37
The News-Boy's Dream of the New Year	40
The Old Church on the Hill	43
The urning of Chicago	45
The Legend of the New Year	48
By the Sea Shore at Night	53
Resurgam	56
Written in a Cemetery	58
Marguerite	60
The Watch-Light	62
New Year, 1868	64

CONTENTS.

	PAGE.
Thanksgiving	66
Miserere	68
Beyond	70
The Sabbath of the Woods	73
A Valentine	76
Snow-Drops	78
Easter Bells	82
In the Sierra Nevada	84
Summer Rain	86
A Baby's Death	88
Christmas	90
My Garden	92
River Song	94
The Return	96
Voices of Hope	99
In the Country	102
Science, the Iconoclast	104
What the Owl said to me	108
Our Volunteers	109
Night: A Phantasy	111
A Monody	113
Minnie	115
The Golden Wedding	118
Verses Written in Mary's Album	121
The Woods in June	123
The Isle of Sleep	126
The Battle Autumn of 1862	130
In War Time	134
Christmas Hymn	137
Te Deum Laudamus	139
A November Wood Walk	141
Resignation	143

CONTENTS.

	PAGE.
Euthanasia	144
Ballad of the Mad Ladye	147
The Coming of the King	150
With a Bunch of Spring Flowers	155
The Higher Law	157
May	158
Two Windows	159
The Meeting of Spirits	161
George Brown	165
Forgotten Songs	169
To the Daughter of the Author of " Violet Keith "	170
A Prelude, and a Bird's Song	172

A little bird woke singing in the night,
  Dreaming of coming day,
And piped, for very fulness of delight,
  His little roundelay.

Dreaming he heard the wood-lark's carol loud,
  Down calling to his mate,
Like silver rain out of a golden cloud,
  At morning's radiant gate.

And all for joy of his embowering woods,
  And dewy leaves he sung,—
The summer sunshine, and the summer floods
  By forest flowers o'erhung.

Thou shalt not hear those wild and sylvan notes
  When morn's full chorus pours
Rejoicing from a thousand feathered throats,
  And the lark sings and soars,

Oh poet of our glorious land so fair,
  Whose foot is at the door :
Even so my song shall melt into the air,
  And die and be no more.

But thou shalt live, part of the nation's life ;
  The world shall hear thy voice
Singing above the noise of war and strife,
  And therefore I rejoice !

THE COMING OF THE PRINCESS.

I.

Break dull November skies, and make
A sunshine over wood and lake;
And fill your cells of frosty air
With thousand, thousand welcomes to the Princely pair!
The land and the sea are alight for them;
The wrinkled face of old Winter is bright for them;
The honour and pride of a race
Secure in their dwelling place,
Steadfast and stern as the rocks that guard her,
Tremble and thrill and leap in their veins,
As the blood of one man through the beacon-lit border!
Like a fire, like a flame,
At the sound of her name,
As the smoky-throated cannon mutter it,
As the smiling lips of a nation utter it,
And a hundred rock-lights write it in fire!
Daughter of Empires, the Lady of Lorne,
Back through the mists of dim centuries borne,
None nobler, none gentler that brave name have worn;
Shrilled by storm-bugles, and rolled by the seas,
  Louise!
Our Princess, our Empress, our Lady of Lorne!

II.

And the wild, white horses with flying manes
Wind-tost, the riderless steeds of the sea,
Neigh to her, call to her, dreadless and free,
" Fear not to follow us; these thy domains;
Welcome, welcome, our Lady and Queen!
O Princess, oh daughter of kingliest sire!
Under its frost girdle throbbing and keen,
A new realm awaits thee, loyal and true!"
And the round-cheeked Tritons, with fillets of blue
Binding their sea-green and scintillant hair,
Blow thee a welcome; their brawny arms bear
Thy keel through the waves like a bird through the air.

III.

Shoreward the shoal of mighty shoulders lean
Through the long swell of waves,
Reaching beyond the sunset and the hollow caves,
And the ice-girdled peaks that hold serene
Each its own star, far out at sea to mark
Thy westward way, O Princess, through the dark.
The rose-red sunset dies into the dusk,
The silver dusk of the long twilight hour,
And opal lights come out, and fiery gleams
Of flame-red beacons, like the ash-gray husk
Torn from some tropic blossom bursting into flower,
Making the sea bloom red with ruddy beams.

IV.

Still nearer and nearer it comes, the swift sharp prow
Of the ship above, and the shadow-ship below,
With the mighty arms of the Tritons under,
All bowed one way like a field of wind-blown ears;
Still nearer and nearer, and now
It touches the strand, and, lo,
With the length of her bright hair backward flowing
Around her head like an aureole,
Like a candle flame in the wind's breath blowing,
Stands she fair and still as a disembodied soul,
With hands outstretched, and eyes that shine through
  tears
And tremulous smiles.
Then the trumpets, and the guns, and the great drums roll,
And the long fiords and the forelands shake with the
  thunder
Of the shout of welcome to the daughter of the Isles!

V.

Bring her, O people, on the shoulders of her vassals
Throned like a queen to her palace on the height,
Up the rocky steeps where the fir-tree tassels
Nod to her, and touch her with a subtle, vague delight,
Like a whisper of home, like a greeting and a smile
From the fir-tree walks and gardens, the wood-embowered
  castles

In the north among the clansmen of Argyle.
Now the sullen plunge of waves for many a mile
Along the roaring Ottawa is heard,
And the cry of some wood bird,
Wild and sudden and sweet,
Scared from its perch by the rush and trample of feet,
And the red glare of the torches in the night.
And now the long façade gay with many a twinkling light
Reaches hands of welcome, and the bells peal, and the guns,
And the hoarse blare of the trumpets, and the throbbing of the drums
Fill the air like shaken music, and the very waves rejoice
In the gladness, and the greeting, and the triumph of their voice.

VI.

Under triumphal arches, blazoned with banners and scrolls,
And the sound of a People's exulting, still gathering as it rolls,
Enter the gates of the city, and take the waiting throne,
And make the heart of a Nation, O Royal Pair, your own.
Sons of the old race, we, and heirs of the old and the new;
Our hands are bold and strong, and our hearts are faithful and true;

Saxon and Norman and Celt, one race of the mingled blood
Who fought, built cities and ships, and stemm'd the unknown flood
In the grand historic days that made our England great,
When Britain's sons were steadfast to meet or to conquer fate.
Our sires were the minster builders, who wrought, themselves unknown,
The thought divine within them, till it blossomed into stone;
Forgers of swords and of ploughshares, reapers of men and of grain,
Their bones and their names forgotten on many a battle plain;
For faith and love and loyalty were living and sacred things,
When our sires were those who wrought, and yours were the leaders and kings.

VII.

For, since the deeds that live in Arthur's rhyme,
Who left the stainless flower of knighthood for all time,
Down to our Blameless Prince, wise, gentle, just,
Whom the world mourns, not by your English dust
More precious held, more sacredly enshrined,
Than in each loyal breast of all mankind,

Men bare the head in homage to the good,
And she who wears the crown of womanhood,
August, not less than that of Empress, reigns
The crowned Victoria of the world's domains!
North, South, East, West, O Princess fair, behold
In this new world, the daughter of the old,
Where ribs of iron bar the Atlantic's breast,
Where sunset mountains slope into the west,
Unfathomed wildernesses, valleys sweet,
And tawny stubble lands of corn and wheat,
And all the hills and lakes and forests dun,
Between the rising and the setting sun;
Where rolling rivers run with sands of gold,
And the locked treasures of the mine unfold
Undreamed of riches, and the hearts of men,
Held close to nature, have grown pure again.
Like that exalted Pair, beloved, revered,
By princely grace, and truth and love endeared,
Here fix your empire in the growing West,
And build your throne in each Canadian breast,
Till West and East strike hands across the main,
Knit by a stronger, more enduring chain,
And our vast Empire become one again.

BIRD SONG.

Art thou not sweet,
Oh world, and glad to the inmost heart of thee!
All creatures rejoice
With one rapturous voice,
As I, with the passionate beat
Of my over-full heart feel thee sweet,
And all things that live, and are part of thee!

Light, light as a cloud
Swimming, and trailing its shadow under me
I float in the deep
As a bird-dream in sleep,
And hear the wind murmuring loud,
Far down, where the tree-tops are bowed,—
And I see where the secret place of the thunders be

Oh! the sky free and wide,
With all the cloud-banners flung out in it
Its singing wind blows
As a grand river flows,
And I swim down its rythmical tide,
And still the horizon spreads wide,
With the birds' and the poets' songs like a shout in it!

BIRD SONG.

Oh life, thou art sweet!
Sweet—sweet to the inmost heart of thee!
 I drink with my eyes
 Thy limitless skies,
And I feel with the rapturous beat
Of my wings thou art sweet,—
And I,—I am alive, and a part of thee!

AN IDYL OF THE MAY.

In the beautiful May weather,
   Lapsing soon into June ;
   On a golden, golden day
   Of the green and golden May,
     When our hearts were beating tune
     To the coming feet of June,
Walked we in the woods together.

   Silver fine
     Gleamed the ash buds through the darkness
     of the pine,
And the waters of the stream
Glance and gleam,
Like a silver-footed dream—
   Beckoning, calling,
   Flashing, falling,
Into shadows dun and brown
   Slipping down,
Calling still—Oh hear! Oh follow !
   Follow—follow !

Down through glen and ferny hollow,
Lit with patches of the sky,
Shining through the trees so high,
Hand in hand we went together,
In the golden, golden weather
    Of the May;
While the fleet wing of the swallow
Flashing by, called—follow—follow!
    And we followed through the day:
    Speaking low—
Speaking often not at all
To the brooklet's crystal call,
    With our lingering feet and slow—
Slow, and pausing here and there
    For a flower, or a fern,
For the lovely maiden-hair;
Hearing voices in the air,
    Calling faintly down the burn.
Still the streamlet slid away,
    Singing, smiling, dimpling down
    To a mossy nook and brown,
Under bending boughs of May;
Where the nodding wind-flower grows,
    And the coolwort's lovely pink,
    Brooding o'er the brooklet's brink
Dips and blushes like a rose.

And the faint smell of the mould,
   Sweeter than the musky scent
Of the garden's manifold
   Perfumes into perfect blent.
Lights and sounds and odours stole,
   In the golden, golden weather—
Heart and thought, and life and soul,
    Stole away,
   In that merry, merry May,
Wandering down the burn together.

Ah Valentine—my Valentine!
Heard I, with my hand in thine,
Grave and low, and sweet and slow,
As the wood bird over head,
Brooding notes, half sung half said,—
"In the world so bleak and wide,
   Hearts make Edens of their own;
Wilt thou linger by my side,—
   Wilt thou live for me alone,
Making bright the winter weather,
   Thou and I and love together?"

"Yea," I said, "for thee alone,"—
   Shading eyes lest they confess
   Too much their own happiness,
With the happy tears o'erflown,

Gravely thou—" The world is not
    Like this ferny hollow :—
Through a rougher, thornier lot
    Wilt thou bravely follow ? "
Still the brook, with softer flow,
    Called, " Oh hear ! Oh follow !"
" Aye," I said, with bated breath,
" Where thou goest, I will go ;
    Holding still thy stronger hand,
    Through the dreariest desert land,
    True, till death."

Silence fell between us two,
Noiseless as the silver dew ;
Hearts that had no need of speech
In the silence spoke to each ;
And along the sapphire blue,
Shot with shafts of sunset through,
Fell a voice, a bodiless breath—
    " True, till death."

Through a mist of smiles and tears,
    Doubts and fears, and toils and dreams,
    Oh ! how long ago it seems,
Looking back across the year
Silver threads are in my hai

And the sunset shadows slope
Back along the hills of hope
That before us shone so fair.
Ah! for us the merry May
Comes no more with golden weather;
Fields, and woods, and sunshine gay,
Purple skies, and purple heather.
We have had our holyday,
And I sit with folded hands,
In the twilight looking back
Over life's uneven track—
Thorny wilds, and desert sands.
Weary heart, unwearied faith,
In the twilight softly saith—
"We have had our golden weather.—
We have walked through life together,
True, till death!"

THE BURIAL OF THE SCOUT.

O not with arms reversed,
And the slow beating of the muffled drum,
And funeral marches, bring our hero home !
These stormy woods where his young heart was nursed
    Ring with a trumpet burst
Of jubilant music, as if he who lies
    With shrouded face, and lips all white and dumb,
Were a crowned conqueror entering paradise,—
    This is his welcome home !

Along the reedy marge of the dim lake,
    I hear the gathering horsemen of the North ;
The cavalry of night and tempest wake,—
    Blowing keen bugles as they issue forth,
To guard his homeward march in frost and cold,
    A thousand spearmen bold !

And the deep-bosomed woods,
With their dishevelled locks all wildly spread,
Stretch ghostly arms to clasp the immortal dead,
    Back to their solitudes :
While through their rocking branches overhead,
    And all their shuddering pulses underground

A shiver runs, as if a voice had said—
    And every farthest leaf had felt the wound—
    He comes—but he is dead!

    The dainty-fingered May
With gentle hand shall fold and put away
    The snow-white curtains of his winter tent,
And spread above him her green coverlet,
    'Broidered with daisies, sweet to sight and scent:
And Summer, from her outposts in the hills,
    Under the boughs with heavy night-dews wet,
Shall place her gold and purple sentinels,
    And in the populous woods sound reveillé,
Calling from field and fen her sweet deserters back—
    But he,—no long roll of the impatient drum,
Nor battle trumpet eager for the fray,
    From the far shores of blue Lake Erie blown,
Shall rouse the soldier's last long bivouac.

QUESTIONINGS.

I touch but the things which are near;
  The heavens are too high for my reach:
    In shadow and symbol and creed,
    I discern not the soul from the deed,
  Nor the thought hidden under, from speech;
And the thing which I know not I fear.

I dare not despair nor despond,
  Though I grope in the dark for the dawn:
    Birth and laughter, and bubbles of breath,
    And tears, and the blank void of death,
  Round each its penumbra is drawn,—
I touch them,—I see not beyond.

What voice speaking solemn and slow,
  Before the beginning for me,
    From the mouth of the primal First Cause,
    Shall teach me the thing that I was,
  Shall point out the thing I shall be,
And show me the path that I go?

Were there any that missed me, or sought,
  In the cycles and centuries fled,

Ere my soul had a place among men ?—
Even so, unremembered again
I shall lie in the dust with the dead,
And my name shall be heard not, nor thought.

Yea rather,—from out the abyss,
  Where the stars sit in silence and light,
  When the ashes and dust of our world
  Are like leaves in their faces up-whirled,—
What orb shall look down through the night,
And take note of the quenching of this ?

Yea, beyond—in the heavens of space
  Where Jehovah sits, absolute Lord,
  Who made out of nothing the whole
  Round world, and man's sentient soul—
Will He crush, like a creature abhorred,
What He fashioned with infinite grace

In His own awful image, and made
  Quick with the flame of His breath,—
  Which He saw and behold it was good ?—
  Ah man ! thou hast waded through blood
And crime down to darkness and death,
Since thou stood'st before Him unafraid.

*   *   *   ✧   *   *

QUESTIONINGS.

My life falls away like a flower
   Day by day,—dispersed of the wind
      Its vague perfume, nor taketh it root,
      Ripening seeds for the sower, or fruit
      To make me at one with my kind,
   And give me my work, and my hour.

No creed for my hunger sufficed,
   Though I clung to them, each after other,
      They slipped from my passionate hold,—
      The prophets, the martyrs of old,—
   Thy pitying face, Mary Mother,—
Thy thorn-circled forehead, O Christ!

Pilgrim sandalled, the deserts have known
   The track of my wandering feet,
      Where dead saints and martyrs have trod,
      To search for the pure faith of God,
   Making life with its bitterness sweet,
And death the white gate to a throne.

O Thou, who the wine-press hast trod,
   O sorrowful—stricken—betrayed,—
      Thy cross o'er my spirit prevails:
      In Thy hands with the print of the nails,
   My life with its burdens is laid,—
O Christ—Thou art sole—Thou art God!

PANSIES.

When the earliest south winds softly blow
Over the brown earth, and the waning snow
In the last days of the discrownèd March,—
Before the silver tassels of the larch,
Or any tiniest bud or blade is seen ;
Or in the woods the faintest kindling green,
   And all the earth is veiled in azure mist,
Waiting the far-off kisses of the sun,—
They lift their bright heads shyly one by one,
   And offer each, in cups of amethyst,
Drops of the honey wine of fairy land,—
A brimming beaker poised in either hand
Fit for the revels of King Oberon,
With all his royal gold and purple on :
Children of pensive thought and airy fancies,
Sweeter than any poet's sweetest stanzas ;
   Though to the sound of eloquent music told,
     Or by the lips of beauty breathed or sung :
They thrill us with their backward-looking glances,
   They bring us to the land that ne'er grows old,—
     They mind us of the days when life was young
Nor time had stolen the fire from youth's romances,
     Dear English pansies !

While still the hyacinth sleeps on securely,
And every lily leaf is folded purely,
   Nor any purple crocus hath arisen;
Nor any tulip raised its slender stem,
   And burst the earth-walls of its winter prison,
And donned its gold and jewelled diadem :
Nor by the brookside in the mossy hollow,
That calls to every truant foot to follow,
   The cowslip yet hath hung its golden ball,—
In the wild and treacherous March weather,
The pansy and the sunshine come together,
   The sweetest flower of all!

   The sweetest flower that blows;
   Sweeter than any rose,
Or that shy blossom opening in the night,
Its waxen vase of aromatic light—
A sleepy incense to the winking stars;
   Nor yet in summer heats,
   That crisp the city streets,—
Where the spiked mullein grows beside the bars
In country places, and the ox-eyed daisy
Blooms in the meadow grass, and brooks are lazy,
And scarcely murmur in the twinkling heat;
When sound of babbling water is so sweet,
   Blue asters, and the purple orchis tall,

Bend o'er the wimpling wave together ;—
The pansy blooms through all the summer weather,
　The sweetest flower of all !

　The sweetest flower that blows !
When all the rest are scattered and departed,
The symbol of the brave and faithful-hearted,
　Her bright corolla glows.
When leaves hang pendant on their withered stalks,
Through all the half-deserted garden walks ;
　And through long autumn nights,
The merry dancers scale the northern heights,
And tiny crystal points of frost-white fire
Make brightly scintillant each blade and spire,
　Still under shade of shelt'ring wall,
Or under winter's shroud of snows,
Undimmed, the faithful pansy blows,
　The sweetest flower of all !

NOVEMBER METEORS.

Out of the dread eternities,
    The vast abyss of night,
A glorious pageant rose and shone,
    And passed from human sight.
We saw the glittering cavalcade,
    And heard inwove through all,
Faint and afar from star to star,
    The sliding music fall.

With banners and with torches,
    And hoofs of glancing flame;
With helm and sword and pennon bright
    The long procession came.
And all the starry spaces,
    Height above height outshone;
And the bickering clang of their armour rang
    Down to the farthest zone.

As if some grand cathedral,
    With towers of malachite,
And walls of more than crystal clear,
    Rose out of the solid light;

And under its frowning gateway,
　Each morioned warrior stept,
And in radiant files down the ringing aisles,
　The martial pageant swept.

From out the oriel windows,
　From vault, and spire, and dome,
And sparkling up from base to cope,
　The light and glory clomb.
They knelt before the altar,
　Each mailed and visored knight,
And the censers swung as a voice outrung,—
　' Now God defend the right ' !

On casque, and brand, and corselet
　Fell the red light of Mars,
As forth from the minster gates they passed
　To the battle of the stars.
Across moon-lighted depths of space,
　And breadths of purple seas,
Their flying squadrons sailed in fleets,
　Of fiery argosies :

Down lengths of shining rivers,
　Past golded-sanded bars,
And nebulous isles of amethyst,
　They dropt like falling stars :

Till on a scarped and wrinkled coast,
    Washed by dark waves below,
They came upon the glittering tents—
    The city of the foe.

Then rushed they to the battle;
    Their bright hair blazed behind,
As deadlier than the bolt they fell,
    And swifter than the wind.
And all the stellar continents,
    With that fierce hail thick sown,
Recoiled with fear, from sphere to sphere
    To Saturn's ancient throne.

The blind old king, in ermine wrapt,
    And immemorial cold,
Awoke, and raised his aged hands,
    And shook his rings of gold.
Down toppled plume and pennon bright,
    In endless ruin hurled;
Their blades of light struck fire from night—
    Their splendours lit the world!

And rolling down the hollow spheres,
    The mighty chords, the seven,
Clanged on from orb to orb, and smote
    Orion in mid-heaven.

Along the ground the white tents lay;
    And faint along the fields.
The foe's swart hosts, like glimmering ghosts,
    Followed his chariot wheels.

With banners and with torches,
    And armour all aflame,
The victors and the vanquished went,
    Departing as they came;
With here and there a rocket sent
    Up from some lonely barque:
Into the vast abysm they passed,—
    Into the final dark.

PICTURES IN THE FIRE.

The wind croons under the icicled eaves,—
    Croons and mutters a wordless song;
And the old elm chafes its skeleton leaves
    Against the windows all night long.

Under the spectral garden wall,
    The drifts creep steadily high and higher
And the lamp in the cottage lattice small
    Twinkles and winks like an eye of fire.

But I see a vision of summer skies,
    Growing out of the embers red,
Under the lids of my half-shut eyes,
    With my arms crossed idly under my head.

I see a stile, and a roadside lime,
    With buttercups growing about its feet,
And a footpath winding a sinuous line
    In and out of the billowy wheat.

For long ago in the summer noons,
    Under the shade of that trysting tree,
My love brought wheat ears and clover blooms,
    And vows that were sweeter than both, to me.

Reading the "Times" in his easy chair,
 With his slippered feet on the fender bright,
Little, I wot, he dreams how fair
 Are the pictures I see in the fire to-night.

Still the wind pipes under the serried spears
 Of frozen boughs a desolate rhyme,
But I hear the rustle of golden ears,
 And in my heart it is summer time.

A MADRIGAL.

The lily-bells ring underground,
   Their music small I hear.
When globes of dew that shine pearl-round
   Hang in the cowslip's ear :
And all the summer blooms and sprays
   Are sheathèd from the sun ;
And yet I feel in many ways
   Their living pulses run.

The crowning rose of summer time
   Lies folded on its stem,
Its bright urn holds no honey-wine,
   It's brow no diadem ;
And yet my soul is inly thrilled,
   As if I stood anear
Some legal presence unrevealed,
   The queen of all the year.

Oh Rose, dear Rose ! the mist and dew
   Uprising from the lake,
And sunshine glancing warmly through,
   Have kissed the flowers awake :—
The orchard blooms are dropping balm,
   The tulip's gorgeous cup
More slender than a desert palm
   It's chalice lifteth up :

A MADRIGAL.

The birds are mated in the trees,
    The wan stars burn and pale,—
Oh Rose, come forth!—upon the breeze
    I hear the nightingale.
Unfold the crimson waves that lie
    In darkness rosy dim,
And swing thy fragrant censer high,
    Oh royal Rose for him!

The hyacinths are in the fields
    With purple splendours pale,
Their sweet bells ring responsive peals
    To every passing gale:
And violets bending in the grass
    Do hide their glowing eyes,
When those enchanting voices pass,
    Like airs from Paradise.

We crowned our blushing Queen of May.
    Long since, with dance and tune;
But the merry world of yesterday
    Is lapsing into June:—
Thou art not here,—we look in vain,—
    Oh Rose, arise, appear!—
Resume thine emerald throne, and reign
    The queen of all the year!

THE PLOUGHBOY.

I wonder what he is thinking
    In the ploughing field all day.
He watches the heads of his oxen,
    And never looks this way.

And the furrows grow longer and longer,
    Around the base of the hill,
And the valley is bright with the sunset,
    Yet he ploughs and whistles still.

I am tired of counting the ridges,
    Where the oxen come and go,
And of thinking of all the blossoms
    That are trampled down below.

I wonder if ever he guesses
    That under the ragged brim
Of his torn straw hat I am peeping
    To steal a look at him.

The spire of the church and the windows
    Are all ablaze in the sun.
He has left the plough in the furrow,
    His summer day's work is done.

And I hear him carolling softly
  A sweet and simple lay,
That we often have sung together,
  While he turns the oxen away.

The buttercups in the pasture
  Twinkle and gleam like stars.
He has gathered a golden handful,
  A leaning over the bars.

He has shaken the curls from his forehead,
  And is looking up this way,—
O where is my sun-bonnet, mother?
  He was thinking of me all day,—

And I'm going down to the meadow,
  For I know he is waiting there,
To wreathe the sunshiny blossoms
  In the curls of my yellow hair.

THE VOICE OF MANY WATERS.

Oh Sea, that with infinite sadness, and infinite yearning
Liftest thy crystal forehead toward the unpitying stars,—
Evermore ebbing and flowing, and evermore returning
Over thy fathomless depths, and treacherous island bars :—

Oh thou complaining sea, that fillest the wide void spaces
Of the blue nebulous air with thy perpetual moan,
Day and night, day and night, out of thy desolate places—
Tell me thy terrible secret, oh Sea! what hast thou done!

Sometimes in the merry mornings, with the sunshine's
  golden wonder
Glancing along thy cheek, unwrinkled of any wind,
Thou seemest to be at peace, stifling thy great heart under
A face of absolute calm,—with danger and death behind!

But I hear thy voice at midnight, smiting the awful silence
With the long suspiration of thy pain suppressed ;
And all the blue lagoons, and all the listening islands
Shuddering have heard, and locked thy secret in their
  breast!

Oh Sea! thou art like my heart, full of infinite sadness
  and pity,—
Of endless doubt and endeavour, of sorrowful question
  and strife,
Like some unlighted fortress within a beleagured city,
Holding within and hiding the mystery of life.

THE DEATH OF AUTUMN.

Discrowned and desolate,
And wandering with dim eyes and faded hair,
Singing sad songs to comfort her despair,
    Grey Autumn meets her fate.

Forsaken and alone
She haunts the ruins of her queenly state,
Like banished Eve at Eden's flaming gate,
    Making perpetual moan.

Crazed with her grief she moves
Along the banks of the frost-charmèd rills,
And all the hollows of the wooded hills,
    Searching for her lost loves.

From verdurous base to cope,
The sunny hill-sides, and sweet pasture lands,
Where bubbling brooks reach ever-dimpled hands
    Along the amber slope,—

And valleys drowsed between,
In the rich purple of the vintage time,
When cups of gold that drop with fragrant wine,
    From orchard branches lean;—

THE DEATH OF AUTUMN.

And far beyond them, spread
Broad fields thick set with sheaves of yellow wheat,
Where scarlet poppies, slumberously sweet,
    Glow with a dusky red—

To the remotest zone
Of hazy woodland pencilled on the sky,
On whose far spires the clouds of sunset lie,—
    She held her regal throne!

Queen of a princely race,
Whose ministers were all the elements;
Sunshine, and rain, and dew she did dispense
    With a right royal grace.

Now, not a breath of air,
Nor sunbeam, nor the voice of beast or bird,
Stirring the lonely woods, hath any word
    To comfort her despair.

Insidious, day by day
A smouldering flame, a lurid crimson creeps
Into the ashy whiteness of her cheeks,
    And burns her life away.

The cavernous woods are dumb!
Through their oracular depths and secret nooks,

To the mute supplication of her looks
    No mystic voices come.

    And through the still grey air
The night comes down, and hangs her lamp on high,
Like a wan lily blossomed on the sky,
    Shining so ghostly fair.

    Or looming up the heights,
Those awful spectres of the frozen zone
Splinter the crystal of heaven's sapphire dome,
    With arrowy-glancing lights.

    The while hoarse night winds rave,
The old year looking backward to his prime
With dim fond eyes, down the last steps of time
    Goes maundering to his grave!

A FAREWELL.

Down the steep west unrolled,
   I watch the river of the sunset flow,
With all its crimson lights, and gleaming gold,
   Into the dusk below.

And even as I gaze,
   The soft lights fade,—the pageant gay is o'er,
And all is grey and dark, like those lost days,
   The days that are no more.

No more through whispering pines,
   I shall behold, in the else silent even,
The first faint star-watch set along the lines
   Of the white tents of heaven.

Before the earliest buds
   Have softly opened, heralding the May
With tender light illuming the gray woods,
   I shall be gone away.

Ah! wood-walks winding sweet
   Through all the valleys sloping to the west,
Where glad brooks wander with melodious feet,
   In musical unrest,—

A FAREWELL.

Ye will not miss me here
   With all the bright things of the coming May,
And the rejoicing of the awakened year,—
   I shall be far away.

Yet in your loneliest nooks,
   I know where all the greenest mosses grow,
And where the violets lift their first sweet looks,
   Out of the waning snow.

And I have heard, unsought,
   Under the musing shadows of the beech,
Wood-voices answering my unspoken thought,
   In half-articulate speech.

And oh! ye shadowy bands,
   Rank above rank along yon rocky height,
That lift into the heavens your mailèd hands,
   And linkèd armour bright.

What other eyes will trace
   From this dear window haunted with the past,
Strange likeness to some well beloved face,
   Among your profiles vast?

What stranger hands will tend
   The nameless treasures I must leave behind,—
My flowers, my birds, and each inanimate friend,
   Linked closer than my kind.

A FAREWELL.

These glorious landscapes old,
  Framed in my cottage windows,—hill-sides dun,
With umber shadows lightened to pale gold,
  By touches of the sun,—

Valleys like emeralds set
  Lonely and sweet in the dusk hills afar,
That half enclose them, like a carcanet
  That holds a diamond star:

Will any gentler face,
  Weary and sad sometimes, like mine grow bright
Touched with your simple beauty—in my place,
  My garden of delight?—

I know not,—yet farewell
  Sweet home of mine,—my parting song is o'er,
And stranger forms among your bowers shall dwell,
  Where I return no more.

THE NEWS-BOY'S DREAM OF THE NEW YEAR

Under the bare brown rafters,
  In his garret bed he lay,
And dreamed of the bright hereafters,
  And the merry morns of May.

The snow-flakes slowly sifted
  In through each cranny and seam,
But only the sunshine drifted
  Into the news-boy's dream.

For he dreamed of the brave to-morrows,
  His eager eyes should scan,
When battling with wants and sorrows,
  He felt himself a Man.

He felt his heart grow bolder
  For the struggle and the strife,
When shoulder joined to shoulder,
  In the battle-field of life.

And instead of the bare brown rafters,
  And the snowflakes sifting in,
He saw in the glad hereafters,
  The home his hands should win :

The flowers that grew in its shadow,
    And the trees that drooped above;
The low of the kine in the meadow,
    And the coo of the morning dove.

And dearer and more tender,
    He saw his mother there,
As she knelt in the sunset splendour,
    To say the evening prayer.

His face—the sun had burned it,
    And his hands were rough and hard,
But home, he had fairly earned it,
    And this was his reward!

The morning star's faint glimmer
    Stole into the garret forlorn,
And touched the face of the dreamer
    With the light of a hope new-born.

Oh, ring harmonious voices
    Of New Year's welcoming bells!
For the very air rejoices,
    Through all its sounding cells!

I greet ye! oh friends and neighbours
    The smith and the artizan;
I share in your honest labours,
    A Canadian working-man.

To wield the axe or the hammer,
   To till the yielding soil,
Enroll me under your banner,
   Oh Brotherhood of Toil!

Ring, bells of the brave to-morrows!
   And bring the time more near:
Ring out the wants and the sorrows,
   Ring in the glad New Year!

THE OLD CHURCH ON THE HILL.

Moss-grown and venerable it stands,
From the way-side dust and noise aloof,
And the great elms stretch their sheltering hands
To bless its grey old roof.

About it summer's greenery waves;
The birds build fearless overhead;
Its shadow falls among the graves;
Around it sleep the dead.

The summer sunshine softly takes
The chancel window's pictured gloom;
The moonlight enters too, and makes
The shadow of a tomb.

Along these aisles the bride hath passed,
And brightened, with her innocent grace.
The pensive twilight years have cast
About the holy place.

They brought her here—a tiny maid,
Unweeting any gain or loss,
And on her baby forehead laid
The symbol of the Cross.

And here they brought her once again,
    White-robed, and smiling as she slept;
While lips, that trembled, breathed her name,
    And eyes that saw her wept.

And still, when sunset lights his fire
    Along the gold and crimsoned west,
She sleeps beneath the shadowing spire,
    The cross upon her breast.

I watch it from my lonely cot,
    When stars shine o'er the hallowed ground,
And think there is no sweeter spot,
    The whole wide earth around.

The Sabbath chimes there sink and swim
    Along the consecrated air,
The benediction and the hymn,
    The voice of praise and prayer:

These mingle with the wind's free song,
    The hum of bees, the notes of birds,
And make an anthem sweet and strong
    Of inarticulate words.

There let me rest, when I have found
    The peace of God, the immortal calm,
Where still above my sleep profound,
    Goes up the Sabbath psalm.

THE BURNING OF CHICAGO

Out of the west a voice—a shudder of horror and pity;
Quivers along the pulses of all the winds that blow;—
Woe for the fallen queen, for the proud and beautiful city.
Out of the North a cry—lamentation and mourning and woe.

Dust and ashes and darkness her splendour and brightness cover,
Like clouds above the glory of purple mountain peaks;
She sits with her proud head bowed, and a mantle of blackness over—
She weepeth sore in the night, and her tears are on her cheeks.

The city of gardens and palaces, stately and tall pavilions,
Roofs flashing back the sunlight, music and gladness and mirth,
Whose streets were full of the hum and roar of the toiling millions,
Whose merchantmen were princes, and the honourable of the earth:

Whose traders came from the islands—from far off summer places,

Bringing spices and pearls, and the furs and skins of beasts,
Men from the frozen North, and men with fierce dark faces,
Men of the desert fire, and the untamed life of the East.

Treasures of gems and gold, of statues and flowers and fountains,
Vases of onyx and jasper from Indian emperors sent;
Pictures out of the heart of tropical sunlit mountains,
  Of rocks of porphyry piled at the gates of the Occident

Dusk-brown sons of the forest, hunters of deer and of bison,
  And the almond-eyed child of the sun met in her busy streets,
With waifs from the banks of the Indus, and the ancient river Pison—
  Lands of the date and the palm, and the citron's hoarded sweets.

The surging tide of the prairie rolled its billows of blossom
  Against her mighty walls, and beat at her hundred gates;
The riches of all the world were poured into her bosom,
  Kings were her mighty men, and lords, and potentates.

She sat in her place by the sea, and the swift-sailing ships obeyed her.

Full freighted with corn and wheat their purple sails
    unfurled,
Far-off in the morning land, and the isles beyond the
    equator;
Out of her heaped-up garners she scattered the bread
    of the world.

As her pride and her beauty were perfect, so desolation
    and mourning,
Swift and sudden, and sure her utter destruction came ;
The heavens above were dark with the smoke of her awful
    burning,
And the earth and the sea were lighted with the
    fierceness of her flame.

Behold oh England! oh, Europe! and see is there any
    sorrow
Like her's who sits in silence among her children slain,
Oh, blackness of woe and ruin ! can any future morrow
    Bring back to the shrouded city her glory and crown
    again !

Aye, subtle and wonderful links of human love and pity,
    Ye have bridged the sea of ruin, and spanned it with
    a span !
She shall rise again from her ashes and build a fairer city,
    With a larger faith in God, and the Brotherhood of Man.

THE LEGEND OF THE NEW YEAR.

I dreamed, and lo, I saw in my dream a beautiful gateway,
   Arched at the top, and crowned with turrets lance-windowed and olden,
And sculptured in arabesque, all knotted and woven and spangled;
   A wonderful legend ran, in letters purple and golden
   Written in leaves and blossoms, inextricably intertangled,
A legend I could not resolve, crowning the gate so stately.

Like statues carven and nitched in the front of some old cathedral,
   Four angels stood each in his turret, immovable warders,
   The first with reverend locks snow-white, and a silver volume
   Of beard that twinkled with frost, and hung to the icicled borders
   That fringed his girdle beneath: ancient his look was, and solemn,
Like a wrinkled and bearded saint blessing some worshipping bedral.

As one in a vision wrapped, with his staff he silently
    pointed
To the golden legend written in glittering star-points
    under,
Shining in crystal ferns, and translucent berries of holly.
Yet as I pondered the words of ineffable awe and wonder,
A mist of rainbow brightness obscured them, and hid
    them wholly,
While wrapt in his vision he stood, like a prophet anointed.

Divers, yet lovely the next, a white-armed, golden-haired
    maiden;
Blue were her eyes and sweet, and her garments were
    lily-bordered;
Her hands were full of flowers, and her eyes of innocent
    gladness,
As the ranks of buds and blossoms, of bees and buds
    she ordered,
Each in their several paths. Mine eyes were heavy
    with sadness,
For I read not yet the legend with beauty and mystery
    laden.

Robed and crowned like an empress in some mediæval
    palace,
Stood the third in her place, with glances of sun-lighted
    splendour;

Stately her height and tall as a queen in some antique story,
  With sheaves about her feet, and the tribute which nations render
To her as the lady of Kingdoms; yet underneath the glory
Of that bright legend to her's was like a containing chalice.

Last of the four, in her turret, serene and benignant,
  Sat in the midst of her children and maidens, a household mother;
  Want, and the sons of penury dwell not among her neighbours;
  Full is her heart of love: her hands wipe the tears of another,
  Yet brings she the gold and the pearls of her manifold labours,
To add to that shining legend the grace of her name and her signet.

Fast closed were the gates, and mute in their places the wardens;
  No voice in my longing ear whispered the mystical sentence,
And my heart was heavy, and chilled with the fruitless endeavour.

On this side lay the snow and the wind, like the wail
of repentance,
Moaned in the branches forlorn but through the closed
lattices ever
Drifted a stir and a fragrance of springtime over the
borders.

Then through the stillness of night struck the clash and
the clangor
Of bells that told twelve from the towers of the neigh-
bouring city;
And lo! the great gates were flung wide, and thronged
with the hurrying races—
High and low, rich and poor—and the light of ineffable
pity,
And infinite love shone down and illumined their faces,
Faces of dolor some, of hope, of sorrow, and anger.

Loud clanged the bells from the towers in jubilant rude-
ness,
And like the voice of a multitude rising respondent,
The words of that marvellous legend made vocal the
silence—
The voice of all sentient creatures ascended triumphant,
And all the listening forests, and mountains, and islands
Heard it, and sang it, " He crowneth the Year with His
goodness!'

Praise Him, O sounding seas, and floods! praise Him
 abounding rivers;
 Praise Him, ye flowery months, and every fruitful
 season!
 Praise Him, O stormy wind, and ice, and snow, and
 vapor,
 Ye cattle that clothe the hills, and man with marvellous
 reason;
 Who crowneth the year with goodness, who prospereth
 all thy labour,
Yea, let all flesh bless the Lord, and magnify Him forever!

BY THE SEA-SHORE AT NIGHT.

Oh lapping waves!—oh gnawing waves!—
   That rest not day nor night,—
   I hear ye when the light
Is dim and awful in your hollow caves:—

All day the winds were out, and rode
   Their steeds, your tossing crest,—
   To-night the fierce winds rest,
And the moon walks above them her bright road.

Yet none the less ye lift your hands,
   And your despairing cry
   Up to the midnight sky,
And clutch, and trample on the shuddering sands,

That shrink and tremble even in sleep,
   Out of your passionate reach,
   Afraid of your dread speech,
And the more dreadful silence that ye keep

BY THE SEA-SHORE AT NIGHT.

Oh sapping waves!—oh mining waves!—
   Under the oak's gnarled feet,
   And tower, and village street,
Scooping by stealth in darkness myriad graves;—

What secret strive ye thus to hide,
   A thousand fathoms deep,
   Which the sea will not keep,
And pours, and babbles forth upon her refluent tide?—

I see your torn and wind-blown hair,
   Strewn far along the shore,—
   And lifted evermore
Your white hands tossing in a fierce despair;

And half I deem ye hold below,
   In vast and wandering cell,
   The primal spirits who fell,
Reserved in chains and immemorial woe.

Keep ye, oh waves!—your mystery:—
   The time draws on apace,
   When from before His face,
The heavens and the earth shall flee,
And evermore there shall be no more sea!

RESURGAM.

Into the darkness and the deeps
  My thoughts have strayed, where silence dwells,
Where the old world encrypted sleeps,—
Myriads of forms, in myriad cells,
Of dead and inorganic things,
  That neither live, nor move, nor grow,
  Nor any change of atoms know;
That have neither legs, nor arms, nor wings,
That have neither heads, nor mouths, nor stings,
That have neither roots, nor leaves, nor stems,
To hold up flowers like diadems,
  Growing out of the ground below:
  But which hold instead
  The cycles dead,
And out of their stony and gloomy folds
Shape out new moulds
  For a new race begun;
Shutting within dark pages, furled
  As in a vast herbarium,
  The flowers and balms,

The pines and palms,
The ferns and cones,
All turned to stones
Of all the unknown elder world,
　　As in a wonderful museum,
Ranged in its myriad mummy shelves.
　　　Insects and worms,—
　　　All lower forms
　　　Of fin and scale,
　　　Of gnat and whale,
Fish, bird, and the monstrous mastodon,
The fabulous megatherium,
And men themselves.

Ah, what life is here compressed,
Frozen into endless rest!
Down through springing blades and spires,
　　Down through mines, and crypts, and caves,
　　Still graves on graves, and graves on graves,
Down to earth's most central fires.

The morning stars sang at their birth,
　　In the first beginnings of time.
What voice of dolour or of mirth
　　At their last funeral made moan,—
Ashes to ashes—earth to earth,
　　And stone to stone,—

Chanting the liturgy sublime.
What matter,—in that doom's-day book
  Their place is fixed—their names are writ,
Each in its individual nook,—
  God's eye beholds—remembers it.
When the slow-moving centuries
Have lapsed in the former eternities,—
  When the day is come which we see not yet,—
When the sea gives up its dead—
  And the thrones are set,
These books shall be opened and read!

WRITTEN IN A CEMETERY.

Stay yet awhile, oh flowers!—oh wandering grasses,
   And creeping ferns, and climbing, clinging vines;—
Bend down and cover with lush odorous masses
    My darling's couch, where he in sleep reclines.

Stay yet awhile;—let not the chill October
   Plant spires of glinting frost about his bed;
Nor shower her faded leaves, so brown and sober,
    Among the tuberoses above his head.

I would have all things fair, and sweet, and tender,—
   The daisy's pearl, the cowslip's shield of snow,
And fragrant hyacinths in purple splendour,
    About my darling's grassy couch to grow.

Oh birds!—small pilgrims of the summer weather,
   Come hither, for my darling loved ye well;—
Here floats the thistle down for you to gather,
    And bearded grasses ripen in the dell.

Here pipe, and plume your wings, and chirp and flutter,
  And swing, light-poised upon the pendant bough ;—
Fondly I deem he hears the calls ye utter,
  And stirs in his light sleep to answer you.

Oh wind!—that blows through wakeful nights and lonely,
  Oh rain !—that sobs against my window pane,—
Ye beat upon my heart, which beats but only
  To clasp and shelter my lost lamb again.

Peace—peace, my soul :—I know that in another
  And brighter land my darling walks and waits,
Where we shall surely meet and clasp each other,
  Beyond the threshold of the shining gates.

MARGUERITE.

Marguerite,—oh Marguerite !
Thy sleep is sound, and still and sweet,
Framed in the pale gold of thy hair,
Thy face is like an angel's fair,
　Marguerite,—oh Marguerite !

Tender curves of cheek and lips—
Sweet eyes hid in long eclipse—
Pale robes flowing to thy feet—
Folded hands that lightly meet,—
　Marguerite,—oh Marguerite !

Sleep'st thou still ?—the world awakes,—
Still the echo swells and breaks,—
Over field, and wood, and street
Easter anthems throb and beat,—
　Marguerite,—oh Marguerite !

Christ the Lord is risen again,—
Hear'st thou not the glad refrain,—

Have those gentle lips no breath,
Smiling in the trance of death?—
　Marguerite,—oh Marguerite!

In the grave from whence He rose,
Lay thee to thy long repose,—
Sweet with myrrh and spices,—sweet
With the footprints of His feet,—
　Marguerite,—oh Marguerite!

Where His sacred head hath lain,
Thine may rest, secure from pain.
While the circling years go round,
Without motion,—without sound,—
　Marguerite,—oh Marguerite!

THE WATCH-LIGHT.

Above the roofs and chimney-tops,
   And through the slow November rain,
   A light from some far attic pane,
Shines twinkling through the water-drops.

Some lonely watcher waits and weeps,
   Like me, the step that comes not yet;—
   Her watch for weary hours is set,
While far below the city sleeps.

The level lamp-rays lay the floors,
   And bridge the dark that lies below,
   O'er which my fancies come and go,
And peep, and listen at the doors;

And bring me word how sweet and plain,
   And quaint the lonely attic room,
   Where she sits singing in the gloom,
Words sadder than the autumn rain.

'A thousand times by sea and shore,
   In my wild dreams I see him lie,
   With face upturned toward the sky,
Murdered, and stiffening in his gore:—

Or drowned, and floating with the tide,
  Within some lonely midnight bay,—
  His arms stretched toward me where he lay,
And blue eyes staring, fixed and wide.

Oh winds that rove o'er land and sea!
  Oh waves that lap the yellow sands!
  Oh hide your stealthy, treacherous hands,
And call no more his name to me.'—

Thus much I heard,—and unawares,
  The sense of pity stole away
  My loneliness and misery,—
When lo, a light step on the stairs!—

Ah joy!—the step that brings my own,
  Safe from all harms and dangers in;—
  My heart lifts up its thankful hymn,
And bids good-night to night and moan.

I sleep,—I rest,—and I forget
  The bridge—the night-lamp's level beams,
  Till waking out of happy dreams,
I see her watch-light shining yet.

God comfort those that watch in vain,—
  I breathe to Him my voiceless prayer;
  Pity their tears and their despair,
And bring the wanderers home again.

NEW YEAR, 1868.

Cradled in ice, and swathed in snows,
And shining like a Christmas rose,
Wreathed round with white chrysanthemums;
   Heaven in his innocent, brave blue eyes,
   Straight from the primal paradise,
Behold the infant New Year comes!

His looks a serious sweetness wear,
   As if upon that unseen way,
Those baby hands that lightly bear
   Garlands, and festive tokens gay,
For but a glance,—a touch sufficed,—
Had met and touched the infant Christ!

And lingering on the wing, had heard,
Sweeter than song of any bird,
Of cherub or of seraphim,
The notes of that divinest hymn,—
Glory to God in highest strain,
And peace on earth, good will to men.

Oh, diamond days, so royally set
   In winter's stern and rugged breast,
Like jewels in an amulet,—
   Your light has cheered, and soothed, and blest,
The want and toil, the sighs and tears,
And sorrows of a thousand years!

NEW YEAR, 1868.

The bells ring in the merry morn,
    The poor forget their poverty,
The saddest face grows bright with glee,
And smiles for joy that he is born;
The fair round world shines out with cheer,
To welcome in the glad New Year.

Oh ye, whose homes are warm and bright,
    With plenty smiling at the board,
Remember those whose roofs to-night,
    Nor warmth, nor light, nor food afford,
Still make those wants, and woes your care,
And let the poor your bounty share.

For yet our hills and lakes along
Echoes the herald angels' song,—
Peace and good will!—oh look abroad,—
    In every nation, tribe, and clan,
    Behold the brotherhood of man,—
Behold the Fatherhood of God!

Peace to our mountains and our hills,—
Peace to our rivers and our rills;—
Our young Dominion takes her place
    Among the nations west and east,—
God send her length of happy days,
    And years of plenty and of peace!

THANKSGIVING.

The Autumn hills are golden at the top,
    And rounded as a poet's silver rhyme;
The mellow days are ruby ripe, that drop
    One after one into the lap of time.

Dead leaves are reddening in the woodland copse,
    And forest boughs a fading glory wear;
No breath of wind stirs in their hazy tops,
    Silence and peace are brooding everywhere.

The long day of the year is almost done,
    And nature in the sunset musing stands,
Gray-robed, and violet-hooded like a nun,
    Looking abroad o'er yellow harvest lands:

O'er tents of orchard boughs, and purple vines
    With scarlet flecked, flung like broad banners out
Along the field paths where slow-pacing lines
    Of meek-eyed kine obey the herdboy's shout;

Where the tired ploughman his dun oxen turns,
  Unyoked, afield, mid dewy grass to stray,
While over all the village church spire burns—
  A shaft of flame in the last beams of day.

Empty and folded are her busy hands;
  Her corn and wine and oil are safely stored,
As in the twilight of the year she stands,
  And with her gladness seems to thank the Lord.

Thus let us rest awhile from toil and care,
  In the sweet sabbath of this autumn calm,
And lift our hearts to heaven in grateful prayer,
  And sing with nature our thanksgiving psalm.

MISERERE.

Be pitiful, oh God! the night is long,
  My soul is faint with watching for the light,
  And still the gloom and doubt of seven-fold night
Hangs heavy on my spirit: Thou art strong:—
  Pity me, oh my God!

I stretch my hands through darkness up to Thee,—
  The stars are shrouded, and the night is dumb;
  There is no earthly help,—to Thee I come
In all my helplessness and misery,—
  Pity me, oh my God!

Be pitiful, oh God!—for I am weak,
  And all my paths are rough, and hedged about,—
  Hold Thou my hand dear Lord, and lead me out,
And bring me to the city which I seek,—
  Pity me, oh my God!

By the temptation which Thou didst endure,
  And by Thy fasting and Thy midnight prayer,
  Jesu! let me not utterly despair;
Oh! hide me in the Rock from ill secure,—
  Pity me, oh my God!

Mine eyes run down with tears that do not cease;
  Oh! when beyond the river dark and cold,
  Shall I the white walls of my home behold,—
  The shining palaces—the streets of gold,—
And enter through the gates the City of Peace,—
  Pity me, oh my God!

BEYOND.

Cloudy argosies are drifting down into the purple dark,
And the long low amber reaches, lying on the horizon's mark,
Shape themselves into the gateways, dim and wonderful unfurled,
Gateways leading through the sunset, out into the underworld.

How my spirit vainly flutters, like a bird that beats the bars,
To be launched upon that ocean, with its tides of throbbing stars,
To be gone beyond the sunset, and the day's revolving zone,
Out into the primal darkness, and the world of the unknown!

Hints and guesses of its grandeur, broken shadows, sudden gleams,
Like a falling star shoot past me, quenched within a sea of dreams,—
But the unimagined glory lying in the dark beyond,
Is to these as morn to midnight, or as silence is to sound.

Sweeter than the trees of Eden, dropping purple blooms,
and balm,
Are the odors wafted toward me from its isles of windless calm,—
And the gold of all our sunsets, with their sapphire all impearled,
Would not match the fused and glowing heaven of that
under world.

Pale sea-buds there weep forever, water lilies damp and
cool,
And the mystic lotus shining through its white waves
beautiful,
In those dusk and sunless valleys, where no steps of mortals tread,
Bind the white brows of the living, whom we blindly
call the dead.

Oh ye lost ones,—ye departed, who have passed that
silent shore,
Though we call you through the sunset, ye return to us
no more.
Have ye found those blessed islands where earth's toils
and sorrows cease?
Do ye wear the sacred lotus,—have ye entered into peace?

Do ye hear us when we call you,—do ye heed the tears we shed,—
Oh beloved!—oh immortal!—oh ye dead who are not dead!
Speak to us across the darkness,—wave to us a glimmering hand,—
Tell us but that ye *remember*, dwellers in the silent land!

But the sunset clouds have faded, arch and capital are gone,
And the regal night is glorious, with the starlight overblown;—
Life is labor and not dreaming, and I have my work to do,
Ere within those happy valleys I shall wear the lilies too.

THE SABBATH OF THE WOODS.

Sundown—and silence—and deep peace,—
Night's benediction and release;—
The tints of day die out and cease.

This morn I heard the Sabbath bells
Across the breezy upland swells;—
My path lay down the woodland dells.

To-day, I said, the dust of creeds,
The wind of words reach not my needs;—
I worship with the birds and weeds.

From height to height the sunbeam sprung,
The wild vine, touched with vermeil, clung,
The mountain brooklet leapt and sung.

The white lamp of the lily made
A tender light in deepest shade,—
The solitary place was glad.

The very air was tremulous,—
I felt its deep and reverent hush,—
God burned before me in the bush!

And nature prayed with folded palm,
And looks that wear perpetual calm,—
The while glad notes uplifted psalm.

The wild rose swung her fragrant vase,
The daisy answered from her place,—
Praise Him whose looks are full of grace.

And violets murmured where the feet
Of brooks made hollows cool and deep;
He giveth His beloved sleep.

Wide stood the great cathedral doors,
Arched o'er with heaven's radiant floors ;—
Nature, with lifted brow, adores.

And wave, and wind, and rocking trees,
And voice of birds, and hum of bees,
Made anthem, like the roll of seas.

The sunset vapors sail and swim ;—
All day uprose their mighty hymn ;—
I listened till the woods were dim.

And through the beechen aisles there fell
A silver silence, like a spell.
The heifer's home returning bell,

Faint and remote, as if it grew
A portion of that silence too,
Dissolved and ceased, like falling dew.

Stars twinkled through the coming night,—
A voice dropped down the purple height,—
At even time it shall be light.

Ah rest my soul, for God is good;
Though sometimes faintly understood,
His goodness fills the solitude.

Fold up thy spirit,—trust the right,
As blossoms fold their leaves at night,
And trust the sun though out of sight.

A VALENTINE.

At last, dear love, the day is gone,
    The doors are barred—the lamps are lit,
The couch beside the fire is drawn,
    The nook where thou wert wont to sit;

The book is open at the place,
    And half its leaves are still uncut,
And yet without thy listening face,
    I cannot read, the book I shut,

And muse, and dream:—it is the day
    When lovers, silent all the year,
Find tongues in floral tokens gay,
    To whisper all they long to hear.

Ah, many a time, and many a time
    I saw the question in thine eyes,
" Where is the silver-sounding rhyme,
    The simple household melodies,

The harp that trembled to thy touch ;
    Hast thou forgot thine early lore ?"
And know'st not that I love so much,
    That song contents my heart no more.

For thou hast made my life so sweet,
    With dainty gifts thy dear hands bring,
Rich with thine affluence, and complete,
    I have no longing left to sing.

And yet, I have such vast desires,
    Such thirst for some great destiny,
That all the poet's weaker fires
    Burn into prophecies for thee.

The circle of our home could make
    The boundaries of my world, but thine
So splendid is,—for thy dear sake,
    I fain would push the bounds of mine.

For this I study as I may
    To walk with thee, the world of mind,
To follow where thou lead'st the way,
    A step,—but just a step behind.

Thy hand in mine, thine earnest eyes
    Fixed ever on the radiant goal,
Together shall we climb the skies,
    And mingle there, one perfect soul.

SNOW-DROPS.

Dimly and dumbly under the ground,
Groping the walls of their prison round,
The roots of the aged and garrulous trees
Are sending electrical messages
    From the under-world to the world without ·
And quickening pulses that course in each
    Fettered and bound and frozen thing,
Rootlets that tremble, and fibres that reach
    Are pushing inanimate fingers out,
To ask in their inarticulate speech
    For tidings of Spring.

And the fine invisible sprite which dwells
In cups and discs, in blossoms and bells,
Fleeter than Ariel's wing hath flown
Beyond this cloudy and frozen zone,
    To the summer land of the South;
Beyond those rugged sentinels
Which winter sets in the snow-capped hills,
    From the breath of whose cruel mouth,
Sighing, the leaves in forest and wold,

Shivered and died in the nights a' cold,
Died and were buried under the snow,
   Long moons ago.

Now over the tropic's broad ellipse
   The sprite hath passed, as fleet and fast
   As the light of falling stars, that cast
A sudden radiance and eclipse ;
   And all the buds that are folded close
   As the inner leaves of an unblown rose,
In bulb, or cone, or scale, or sheath,
And sealed with the odorous gums that breathe
Like the breath of the singing and sighing pine,
When the dews are falling at evening time,
Through cone, and sheath, and bulb, and scale—
   Tremble, and cry All hail !

And look where a rosier beam hath cleft
   The damp and fragrant-smelling earth,
   A handful of snow-drops peeping forth ;
As if King Winter had dropped and left—
Stumbling and tripping the steep hills down—
Had clutched his robe and dropped his crown :
Or as if the very snow had power,
Out of itself to fashion a flower ;
So vase-like, slender, and exquisite,
Like an alabaster lamp alit,—

And shining with a sea-green light,
   As if it had but newly come
Up from some subterranean palace,
   The haunt of fairy or of gnome,
With its waxen taper still alight,
   And beaming in its leafy chalice,
That lit the revellers down below,
When the nights were long, and the moon was low.
You might have heard, far-off and sweet,
   The sound of the elfin revelries,
   Like a bugle strain blown over seas,
And the patter and beat of dancing feet,—
   If you had been like me awake,
   What time the Great Bear seems to shake,
Down through the trackless realms of air,
Frost-lances from his shaggy hair;
And all around—beneath—across,
The round globe lies stabbed through with frost.

   Now the touches of the sun,
Like some potent alchemist,
In heat and dews, in rain and mist,
   As in a subtle menstruum,
Hath dissolved the icy charm,
   And laid on that cold breast of hers,—
   Nature's breast—that faintly stirs,

With his fragaant kisses warm,
Sweet as myrrh and cinnamon,—
 Snow-drops, spring's bright harbingers,
 First-born children of the sun.

Like a sudden burst of leaf and bloom,
The sun shines redly through the gloom,
And the wind with its many melodies
Hath a murmurous sound like the noise of bees,
Singing and humming,—blowing and growing,
Of springing blade, and of fountain flowing;
And night and silence under the ground
Listen—and thrill—and move to the sound,
 And answer, Spring is coming!

EASTER BELLS.

Oh bells of Easter morn, oh solemn sounding bells,
    Which fill the hollow cells
Of the blue April air with a most sweet refrain,
    Ye fill my heart with pain.

For when, as from a thousand holy altar-fires,
    A thousand resonant spires
Sent up the offering—the glad thanksgiving strain—
    "The Lord is risen again!"

He went from us who shall return no more, no more!
    I say the sad words o'er,
And they are mixed and blent with your triumphant psalm,
    Like bitterness and balm,

We stood with him beside the black and silent river,
    Cold, cold and soundless ever;
But there our feet were stayed—unloosed our clasping fond,
    And he has passed beyond.

And still that solemn hymn, like smoke of sacrifice,
    Clomb the blue April skies,
And on our anguish placed its sacramental chrism,
    " Behold, the Lord is risen !"

Oh, bells of Easter morn ! your mighty voices reach
    A deeper depth than speech;
We heard, " Because He liveth *they* shall live with Him;"
    This was our Easter hymn.

And while the slow vibrations swell, and sink, and cease,
    They bring divinest peace,
For we commit our best beloved to the dust,
    In sure and certain trust.

IN THE SIERRA NEVADA.

I lift my spirit to your cloudy thrones,
  And feel it broaden to your vast expanse,
    Oh! mountains, so immeasurably old,
    Crowned with bald rocks and everlasting cold,
  That melts not underneath the sun's fierce glance,
Peak above peak, fixed, dazzling, ice and stones.

Down your steep sides quick torrents leap and roar,
  And disappear, in gloomy gorges sunk,
    Fringed with black pines on dizzy verges high-
    Poised, trembling to the thunder and the cry
  Of the lost waters, through each giant trunk,
And farthest twig and tassel evermore.

Behold far down the mountain herdsman's ranche,
  The rough road winding past his lonely door,
    And in his ears, by day and night, the sound
    Of mad waves plunging down the gulfs profound,
  The tempest's gathering cry, the dull deep roar,
And the long thunder of the avalanche!

IN THE SIERRA NEVADA.

Night broods along the vallies while your peaks
   Are pink and purple with the rays of morn,
     And filmy tints that swim the depths of space,
     To reach, and kiss you first upon the face,
   Before the world awakes, and day is born,
To flush with colder gleam your rugged cheeks.

And last, and longest lingering, the light
   Is on your mighty foreheads, when the sun
     Sets in the sea, and makes a palace fair
     For his repose, of crystal wave and air,—
   Ye seem to stoop, and smile to look upon
The fallen monarch from your silent height.

Vallies are green about your rocky feet,
   And sweet with clambering vines, and waving corn,
     And breath of flowers, and gold of ripening fruit;
     Cities send up their smoke, and man and brute
   Beneath your wide embrazure have been born
And died for ages, yet Ye hold your seat.

I lift my spirit up to you, and seem
   To feel your vastness penetrate my soul ;
     And faintly see, far-off, and looming broad
     And dread, the grandeur of the world of God,
   And thrill to be a part of the great whole,
Which towers above me, a stupendous dream.

SUMMER RAIN.

O rain, Summer Rain! forever,
   Out of the crystal spheres,
And cool from my brain the fever,
   And wash from my eyes the tears.

Stir gently the blossoming clover,
   In the hollows dewy and deep;—
Somewhere they are blossoming over
   The spot where I shall sleep.

Asleep from this wearisome aching,
   With my arms crossed under my head,
I shall hear without awaking,
   The rain that blesses the dead.

And the ocean of man's existence,—
   The surges of toil and care,
Shall break and die in the distance,
   But never reach me there.

And yet—I fancy it often—
   I should stir in my shrouded sleep,
And struggle to rise in my coffin,
   If he came there to weep.

Among the dead—or the angels—
Though ever so faint and dim,
I should know that voice in a thousand,
And stretch my hands to him.

But the trouble of life and living,
And the burden of daily care,
And the endless sin, and forgiving,
Are greater than I can bear.

So rain, Summer Rain, and cover
The meadows dewy and deep,
And freshen the blossoming clover,
And sing me to dreamless sleep.

A BABY'S DEATH.

A little white soul went up to God,
  Out of the mire of the city street;
It grew like a flower in the highway broad,
  Close to the trample of heedless feet.

It fell like a snow-flake over night,
  Into the ways by vile ones trod;
It sparkled—dissolved in the morning light,
  And the little white soul went up to God.

Dainty, flower-soft, waxen thing,
  Its clear eyes opened on this bad earth,
And the little shuddering soul took wing,
  By the gate of death, from the gate of birth.

Not for those innocent lips and eyes,
  The words and the ways of sin and strife;
The pure flower opened in paradise,
  Fast by the banks of the river of life.

Yea, little victors, who never fought;
And crowned, though ye never ran the race,
His blood your innocent lives hath bought,
And ye stand before Him and see His face!

For this, oh Father! we give Thee thanks,
By the little graves, and the tear-wet sod;
They stand before Thee in shining ranks,
And the little white souls are safe with God!

CHRISTMAS.

The birth-day of the Christ child dawneth slow
    Out of the opal east in rosy flame,
    As if a luminous picture in its frame—
        A great cathedral window, toward the sun
Lifted a form divine, which still below
        Stretched hands of benediction;—while the air
        Swayed the bright aureole of the flowing hair
Which lit our upturned faces;—even so
        Look on us from the heavens, divinest One!
And let us hear through the slow moving years,
Long centuries of wrongs, and crimes, and tears,—
        The echo of the angel's song again,
    Peace and good will, good will and peace to men.
A little space make silence,—that our ears,
        Filled with the din of toil and moil and pain,
May catch the jubilant rapture of the skies,—
The glories of the choirs of paradise.

CHRISTMAS.

The hills still tremble when the thunders cease
  Of the loud diapason,—and again
Through the rapt stillness steals the hymn of peace;
  Melodious and sweet its far refrain
Dying in distance, as the shadows die
Of white wings vanished up the morning sky,
    As farther still—and thinner—more remote—
    A film of sound, the aerial voices float—
Peace and good will, good will and peace to men!

MY GARDEN.

Only the commonest flowers
  Grow in my garden small,
Like buttercups, and bouncing-bets,
  And hollyhocks by the wall;
And sunflowers nodding their stately heads,
  Like grenadiers so tall.
But the purple pansy grows beneath—
  The sweetest flower of all—
And tiny feathery filmy ferns
  You scarce can see at all,
Fleck the shady side of the stones,
  So dainty, fine and small.

Only the commonest flowers
  Grow in this garden of mine,
The larkspur flaunting her sky-blue cap,
  And the twinkling celandine
Shakes her jewels of freckled gold,
  And drinks her honey-wine,
Making a cup of her lucent stem,
  So slender and so fine.

You hear the waves that dimple and slide,
  Slide and shimmer and shine,
Under her fairy-slippered feet—
  My golden celandine.

The hands of the little children
  Gather them without fear;
Wonders of beauty and gladness
  To them my flowers appear.
I have seen them bend to listen,
  With poised and patient ear,
The curfew chime of the fairies,
  In the lily's bell to hear.
Oh, blessed and innocent children,
  With eyes so crystal clear,
That ye look with the dual vision
  Of the baby and the seer.
To you the stars and the angels,
  And the heavens themselves are near,
And the amaranths of paradise,
  That blossom all the year:
I would I could see what ye see,
  And hear what ye can hear.

RIVER SONG

Swift and silent and strong!
   Under the low-browed arches,
Through culverts, and under bridges,
   Sweeping with long forced marches
Down to the ultimate ridges,—
   The sand, and the reeds, and the midges,
And the down-dropping tassels of larches,
   That border the ocean of song.

Swift and silent and deep!
   Through the noisome and smoke-grimed city,
Turning the wheels and the spindles,
   And the great looms that have no pity,—
Weight, and pulley, and windlass,
   And steel that flashes and kindles,
And hears no forest-learnt ditty,
   Not even in dreams and sleep.

Blithe and merry and sweet!
   Over its shallows singing,—
I hear before I awaken
   The sound of the church-bells ringing,

RIVER SONG.

And the sound of the leaves wind-shaken,
Complaining and sun-forsaken,
And the oriole warbling and singing,
And the swish of the wind in the wheat

Sweet and tender and true!
From meadows of blossoming clover,
Where sleepy-eyed cows are lowing,
And bobolinks twittering over,—
Ebbing and falling and flowing—
Singing and gliding and going—
The river—my silver-shod lover,
Down to the infinite blue.

Deep, and tender, and strong!
With resonant voice and hollo—
To far away sunshiny places,
Haunts of the bee and the swallow,
Where the Sabbath is sweet with the praises
Of dumb things, of weeds and of daisies,—
Oh river! I hear thee—I follow
To the ocean where I too belong.

THE RETURN.

I have been where the roses blow,
   Where the orange ripens its gold,
And the mountains stand with their peaks of snow,
   To fence away the cold;
Where the lime and the myrtle lent
   Their fragrance to the air,
To make the land of my banishment
   More exquisitely fair.

And I heard the ring dove call
   To his mate in the blossoming trees,
And I saw the white waves heave and fall.
   Far away over southern seas.
I listened along the beach,
   By the shore of the shifting sea,
To the waves, till I knew their murmured speech,
   And the message they bore to me.

And I watched the great sails furled,
   Like the wings of some ocean bird,
That brought me, out of another world,
   A warning, and a word;

For still beside my way,
 By shore or sunlit wave,
There journeyed with me night and day,
 The shadow of a grave.

Oh, friends! my heart went forth
 To you with a yearning cry,
To be taken back to my native North—
 To be taken home to die.
For sweeter than southern suns,
 Or the blossoms of summer lands,
Are the faces of my little ones,
 And the touch of their tender hands.

Come closer to my side,
 Your eyes are as clear and true
As if they were stars my way to guide,
 My darlings, back to you.
Oh God! my heart is stirred
 With thankfulness and rest,
To reach at last, like a wounded bird,
 The shelter of its nest.

Oh, faint pulse, throbbing long!
 And weary and fluttering breath,
'Twas the mother-love that kept you strong,
 Though face to face with death.

But now my eyes are dim,
    And my breath comes weak and slow,
Sing to me softly the evening hymn,
    And kiss me ere I go.

Come close: for the angel waits—
    The angel with gentle hand,
To open for me the shadowy gates,
    Into the silent land.
Oh, voices sweet and clear!
    What light is in the skies?
Is it your glad voices that I hear—
    Or the hymns of paradise?

Farewell! your faces fade—
    Fade—fade—and disappear
In the light no earthly cloud may shade,
    Heaven's morning dawning clear.
Oh, land of rest so fair!
    By angel footsteps trod,
I shall wait for you, beloved there,
    In the paradise of God.

VOICES OF HOPE.

It is the hither side, O Hope,
And afternoon; our shadows slope
Backward along the mountain cope.

The early morning was so sweet,
We seemed to climb with wingèd feet,
Like moving vapors fine and fleet.

Not more elastic poised and swung
Harebell or yellow adder's tongue,
Nor blither any bird that sung.

Thy light foot bent not any stem
Of frailest plant, whose diadem
In passing kissed thy garment's hem.

O Hope! so near me and so bright,
Thy foot above me on the height,
I might not touch thy garments white.

Thy lifted face, so fair, so rapt,
Like sunshine rolled and overlapped
Cliff, slope, and tall peak thunder-capped.

Thy voice to me like silver brooks
Down dropped from secret mountain nooks,
Still drew me, like thy radiant looks.

Nor scorching sun, nor beating rain,
Nor soil, nor grime, nor travel-stain,
With thee, were weariness or pain.

But now—it is the afternoon
Behind, the mountain summit's gloom:
Before, night's shadows gather soon.

O Hope! where art thou?—rough and steep
The way has grown; I faint and weep,
Beside me torrents toss and leap;

And far below, unseen for tears,
The river where life disappears,
Uplifts its thunder to my ears.

Canst thou, with thy serener eyes,
Over the flood God's paradise,
Behold in awful beauty rise?

Far off I seem to see thee stand,
Shading rapt eyes with radiant hand,
To scan that unknown glorious land.

The glory of that unseen place,
Gathers and brightens o'er thy face,
And fills thy looks with tender grace.

O, Hope divine!—*I* would behold
Those shining spires, those streets of gold:
But ah! the waves are deadly cold!

I hear the thunder and the sweep
Of waves; deep calleth unto deep;
The pathway ends, abrupt and steep.

Yet, soft beside that solemn shore,
I hear thy voice above its roar:
" Life is a dream—and it is o'er;

" The night is past—behold the day,
O new-born soul—O child of clay,
O bird uncaged and still astray ;

" Take through the universe thy road;
All paths lead up to His abode,
Converging at the Mount of God!"

IN THE COUNTRY.

Here the sunshine, filtering down,
Through leaves of emerald, dun and brown,
  Is green instead of golden;
And the hum and roar of the distant town
  In an endless hush is holden.

Twinkling bright through the shadowing limes,
The brook rains a sparkle of silver rhymes
  On the dragon-fly, its neighbour;
It pays no duty in dollars and dimes,
  For its work is all love-labour.

Here are no spindles, nor wheels to be whirled,
No forges nor looms from the outside world,
  Stunning the ear with clamour;
You hear but the whisper of leaves unfurled,
  And the tap of the woodpecker's hammer.

Here are no books to be written or read,
But cushions of softest moss instead,
  Without a care to cumber;
And fern-leaf fans for the weary head,
  Soothing the soul to slumber

Oh! come from the dusty haunts of trade,
From the desk, the ledger, the loom, the spade;
    There is neither toil nor payment,
Forget for once, in this peaceful shade,
The sordid ways in which dollars are made,
    And food and drink and raiment.

Consider the lilies, arrayed so fair,
In robes that an eastern king might wear,
    Though never an eye may heed them;
And the sparrows, of whom His hand takes care,
    For our Father in Heaven feeds them.

His rainbow spans the heavenly blue;
His eye takes note of the drops of dew,
    And the sunset's golden arrows;
And shall He not take thought of you,
    O man, as well as the sparrows?

SCIENCE, THE ICONOCLAST.

> " Oh ! spare those idols of the past,
> Whose lips are dumb, whose eyes are dim ;
> Truth's diadem is not for him
> Who comes, the fierce Iconoclast:
> Who wakes the battle's stormy blast,
> Hears not the angel's choral hymn."
> THE IMAGE-BREAKER.

Ah me ! for we have fallen on evil days,
   When science, with remorseless cold precision,
Puts out the flame of poetry, and lays
   Her double-convex lens on fancy's vision.
When not a star has longer leave to shine,
   Unweighed, unanalysed, reduced to gases,—
Resolved to something in the chemist's line,
   By those miraculously long-ranged glasses.

The awful mysteries which Nature locks
   Deep in her stony bosom, hid for ages,—
The hieroglyphics of primeval rocks,
   Are glibly written out on short-hand pages.
Within that rocky scroll, her palimpsest,
   The hand of time still writes, and still effaces
Records in dolomite—and shale—and schist,
   The pre-historic history of Races.

Cave-dwellers, under nameless strata hid,
  Vast bones of extinct monsters that were fossil,
Ere the first Pharaoh built the pyramid,
  And shaped in stone his sepulchre colossal.
What undiscovered secret yet remains
  Beneath the swirl and sway of billows tidal,
Since Art triumphant led the deep in chains,
  And on the mane of ocean laid her bridle.

Into those awful crypts of cycles dead,
  Shrouded and mute, each in its mummy-chamber,
Her daring step intrudes without more dread
  Than to behold a fly embalmed in amber.
Stars—motes—worlds—molecules, and microcosms,
  Her level gaze sweeps down the page recorded,
And withers all its myths, and fairy blossoms,
  Condemned to explanations dull and sordid.

Alike the sculptures of the graceful Greeks,
  Grey with the moss of eld and venerable,
The fauns, the nymphs, the half-defaced antiques,
  The gods and men of mythologic fable,
And legends of steel-casqued and mailèd men,
  The old heroic tales of love and glory,
Of knight, and palmer, and the Saracen,
  And the crusaders of enchanted story;

Grim ghosts and goblins, and more harmless sprites
  That peopled once our juvenile romances,
And made us shiver in our beds o'nights,
  Science has banished those bewitching fancies;
And given us the merest husks instead,
  The very bones and skeleton of nature,
Filling those peaceful hours with shapes of dread,
  And horrid ranks of Latin nomenclature.

Blest is the Indian on his native plains,
  And blest the wandering Tartar, happy nomad,
Fire-worshippers, whose twinkling altar-fanes
  Still gleam on lonely peaks beyond Allahbad.
Shadows yet linger round their ruined towers,
  And whisper from the caverns and the islands,
Their Memnon still is eloquent, but our's
  Stares on with shut lips in an age-long silence.

Not so! The age still ripens for her needs
  The flower, the man. Behold her slow still finger
Points where He comes, beneath whose feet the weeds
  Bloom out immortal flowers, the immortal Singer!
Forward, not backward all the ages press;
  New stars arise, of whose bright occultation
No glory of the dying past could guess:
  Still grows the unfinished miracle, Creation.

Oh ! Poet of the years that are to come,
  Singing at dawn thy idyls sweet and tender—
The preludes of the great millenium
Of song, to drown the world in light and splendour,
Awake, arise ! thou youngest born of time !
  Through flaming sunsets with red banners furled,
The nations call thee to thy task sublime,
  To .ing the new songs of a newer world !

WHAT THE OWL SAID TO ME.

The moon went under a ragged cloud,
    The owl cried out of the ruined wall,
Slow and solemn, distinct and loud,
    His melancholy call :
Tu-whit, tu-whit, tu-whoo !
Like a creature in a shroud.

Across the night in a silver chain,
    While a lonesome wind arose and died,
Slow stepped the ghostly feet of the rain;
    The owl from the wall replied :
Tu-whit, tu-whoo, hoo-hoo !
    With a peal of goblin laughter,
    And silence fell thereafter.

Weird fingers of the wandering rain,
    Reaching out of the hollow dark,
Paused and tapped at my window-pane,—
    A muffled voice cried, Hark !
Tu-whit, tu-whit, tu-whoo !
    The moon is drowned in the dark,
    And the world belongs to me and you !

OUR VOLUNTEERS.

Where shall we write your names, ye brave !
Where build for you a monument,
Who lie in many a sylvan grave,
Stretched half across the continent !
Young, bright and brave, the very flower
And choice of all we had to give,
With you what glory ceased to live,—
Or lives again in hearts of men.
An inspiration and a power !

For when one sunny day in June,
A sudden war-cry shook the land,
As if from out clear skies at noon
Had dropped the lightning's deadly brand :—
Ah then, while rang our British cheers,
And pealed the bugle, rolled the drum,
We saw the Nation rise like one !
Swift formed the files,—a thousand miles
Of them, our gallant Volunteers !

Deep clanged the bells, the drums did beat,
And still from east and west they came ;

Echoed the street with martial feet,
    From north, from south, with hearts aflame:
Ah, still the fires of freedom burn,—
    Be witness, Ridgway's silent shade,
    No foe shall dare our land invade,
    While hearts like those that met the foes,
    Still beat like theirs,—the undismayed,
The brave, who never will return.

Our Country holds them in her heart,
    Shrined with her mountains and her rivers;
    And still for them her proud lip quivers,
And tears to her great eyelids start:
But they are tears of love and pride,
    And she shall tell to coming years
    The story of her Volunteers,
    For all their names are her's and fame's—
The brave who live, the brave who died.

NIGHT.—A PHANTASY.

Night! the horrible wizard Night!
The dumb and terrible Night
Hath drawn his circle of magic, round
Over the sky, and over the ground,
　　Without a sound.
Ah me, what woful phantoms rise,
With ice-cold hands and pitiless eyes,
As stars grow out of the summer skies,
Tangible things to mortal sight,
Under the hands of the wizard Night!

Night! the mystical prophet, Night!
　The haunted and awful Night!
With the trail of his garment's shadowy fall,
Soundless and black as a funeral pall,
Now enters his dread laboratory.
A wan, and faint, and wavering glory
Shines from a veiled lamp somewhere hidden,
　　Like a lily in a grave:
And things unholy, and things forbidden,—
Hands that have long been the earth-worm's prey,

And shrouded faces out of the clay,
Rise and fill the enchanted cave
With a pale and deathly light,—
The haunted and awful Night!

Night! the abhorred magician Night!
The black astrologer Night!
Night is the world!—I shiver with fright:—
The air is full of evil things,
The coil and glitter of snaky rings,
And the tremor of vast invisible wings,
That are not heard but felt:
They touch my hair, my hand, my cheek,
They mope and mouth, but they never speak
To utter their awful history.
Oh, when will the darkness break and melt,
Like blocks of ice on a golden reef,
And little by little, as leaf by leaf,
In light and color and form increased,
The rose of morning blooms in the east,—
The old yet ever new mystery!
And I fall on my knees to worship the light
That casts out the evil demon of Night,
And hallows with blossoms, like prayers, the way
Of another new day.

A MONODY.

On the early and lamented death of George and Maggie Rosseaux, brother and sister, who died within one week of each other in the autumn of 1875. Young, beautiful and beloved, they were indeed lovely and pleasant in their lives, and in their death they were not divided.

Pace slowly, black horses, step stately and solemn—
One by one—two by two—stretches out the long column;
Pass on with your burden, the sound of our tears
    Will not reach the deaf ears.

Beneath the black shadow of funeral arches,
Stepping slow to the rhythm of funeral marches;
Pass on down the street where their steps were so gay,
    And so light, yesterday.

Where it seems if we turn we shall clasp them and hold
    them,
Our hands shall embrace—and our eyes shall behold
    them,—
So near are the confines of hither, and yonder,—
    So world-wide asunder !

H

Oh, lovers and friends! ye were youth and glad weather,
And beauty and strength, and all bright things together;
With the smile on your lips, and the flower at your breast
    Have ye gone to your rest.

The dull lives of others move on, while the splendid
Beginnings of yours are all broken and ended,
The high hopes, the bright dreams, and youth's confident
    trust,
    Gone down to the dust.

Step slowly, black steeds, at the head of the column,
Breathe softly, dead marches, so mournfully solemn;
Ye bear from our sight what no morn shall restore
    Nevermore, nevermore.

Oh, beloved—oh, wept for!—beyond the dark river
Are the lives incomplete, there made perfect forever?
Oh, wave but a hand through the darkness, to tell
    It is well with ye—well.

Profound is the darkness—the silence unbroken—
No glimmer of pale hands comes back as a token:
Yet still in our hearts we have heard the words spoken:—
"He hath overcome death—He hath passed through the
    grave—
    He is able to save."

MINNIE.

"And Jesus called a little child unto him."
MATT. XVIII. 2.

Oh, my blossom, my darling, whose dimpled hands are cold!
Oh, my baby, my treasure, laid under the green mould!
Earth pressed on thy closed eyelids, and on thy sunny hair,
And folded hands, and smiling lips, so exquisitely fair.

Cold and dark are the night dews around thy grassy bed,
Instead of warm and loving arms beneath thy sunny head;
Oh, my blossom, my darling, the long nights through, awake,
I stretch my empty arms for thee,—my heart—my heart will break.

The autumn leaves are falling ungathered on the hill,
The soft October sun is bright, but the little hands are still;

And the little feet that chased them as frolicksome and light,
Have lain beneath them—can it be?—a whole day and a night.

The autumn winds will sigh and moan ; the dreary, dreary rain
Will drench thy lowly pillow, sweet, with tears like mine in vain ;
And weary, weary months drag on, and long years stretch before,
Whilst thou to me, my beautiful, returnest nevermore.

Beyond our earthly vision—beyond the burial sod,
Where the palm trees and the amaranths grow on the hills of God,
Oh, golden gates, that stand within the holy, heavenly place,
Open for me but a little, that I may behold her face.

Open for me but a little, that I may touch her hand,
And hear her sing the hymn she loved about " The Promised Land."
Oh, my blossom ! Oh, my darling ! though it be but in a dream,
Speak to me,—I watch—I listen,—speak to me across the stream.

Kneeling—praying at the threshold—day and night, and
  night and day;
When I rise with heavy eyelids—when I kneel at night
  to pray—
Still I wait to catch the far-off music of thy starry
  hymn,
Till I hear the voice that called thee bid me rise and
  enter in.

THE GOLDEN WEDDING.

Inscribed to OUR FATHER AND MOTHER, and read on that Anniversary, FEBRUARY 15TH, 1876.

A half a century of time,
    The mingled pain and bliss
That make the history of life
    Between that day and this!
Two lives that in that morning light,
    Together were made one,
Now standing where the shadows fall
    Athwart the setting sun.

How long it seems!—the devious way.
    And full of toil and pain,—
Yet love and peace kept house with them,
    And love and peace remain.
Though youth and strength and youthful friends
    Were left upon the road
Long since, an honest man is still
    The noblest work of God.

No famous deeds, no acts achieved
  In battle or in state
Make memorable this festal day,
  The day we celebrate:
Divided from the common lot
  By neither fame nor pelf,
Our hearts revere the man who loves
  His neighbour as himself.

The fragrance of the Christian's life,
  Though humble and unknown,
Is a more precious heritage
  Than heirship to a throne.
That lowly roof—what memories
  Of blessings cluster there,
Around the hearthstone consecrate
  By fifty years of prayer!

The shaded lamp, the cheerful fire,
  Our Mother's patient look,
The firelight on her silver hair,
  And on the Holy Book;—
Where e'er our erring feet may stray,
  The welcome waits the same,—
That light, that look will follow still,
  And soften and reclaim.

THE GOLDEN WEDDING.

Type of the Fatherhood of God,
    Whose love has kept us still,
In all the changeful scenes of life
    Secure from every ill,
And brought our long-divided band,
    Not one of us astray,
Around our Father's board to keep
    This Golden Wedding Day.

Oh ye beloved and revered!
    Our hearts make thankful prayer,
That still around our household hearth
    There is no vacant chair.
God grant that we may be of those
    Who sing the heavenly psalm,
And sit together at the feast,
    The marriage of the Lamb!

VERSES.

WRITTEN IN MARY'S ALBUM.

In your beautiful book, dear Mary,
  With pages so white and fair,
I pause ere I trace the first sentence,
  And thoughtfully breathe a prayer:—

That in the dew of the morning,
  Ere the shadows begin to fall,
You may turn with a child's devotion
  To the Book that is best of all :—

And learn with the gentle Mary,
  - At the Saviour's feet to stay,
And to choose that better portion
  Which shall never be taken away.

Ah! lovely and thrice beloved,
  Sitting at Jesus' feet,
In the shady walks of Bethany,
  And the summer twilight sweet,—

With the thrilling palms and the olives,
  Listening overhead,
To that wonderful voice whose music
  Had power to waken the dead!

Even thus through life's grave-shadowed valleys,
  We may walk with that Heavenly Friend,
With a child's loving faith in His promise
  To be with us unto the end.

So I ask for my Mary, not grandeur,
  Nor the wealth, nor the fame of the day,
But that which the world cannot give her,
  The peace which it takes not away.

THE WOODS IN JUNE.

In the sleep-haunted gloom
Born of the slumbrous twilight in these shades,
These vast and venerable collonades,
    I welcome thee, dear June !

And while with head reclined,
And limbs aweary with my woodland walk,
I listen to the low melodious talk
    Of leaves and singing wind,

The merry roundelay
Of the swart ploughman, sowing summer grain,
And tinkling sheep-bell on the distant plain,
    And pastures far away,

Come with a soft refrain,
Like a faint echo from the outer world,
While Peace sits by me with her white wings furled,
    Within my green domain.

This is my palace, where
Great trunks are amber pillars to support
The blue roof of the vast and silent court,
    In clustered columns fair:

And underneath, the bloom
Of water-lilies through the fragrant night
Of these dim arches spreads a perfumed light,
Even at highest noon.

Down dropping all day long,
With a most musical cadence in the hall,
A wandering stream lets its slow waters fall
In twinkling rhythmic song.

Hither the vagrant bee,
From the broad fields and sunshine all astray,
Loiters the idle hours of noon away,
In golden dreams like me.

And from my window frame,
This oriel window opening on the sky,
I see the white barques of the clouds drift by,
With prows of rosy flame.

Fantastical and strange,
Their purple sails go floating o'er the deep,
Like shadows through the summer land of sleep,
In never ending change.

The wild shy things which roam
The woods, and live in bough and tree and grot,

Flutter and chirp unscared, they fear me not,
 For I too am at home.

 And feel my heart in tune
With the great heart of Nature, and the voice
Of all the glad bright creatures that rejoice
 In the green woods of June.

THE ISLE OF SLEEP.

In those dark mornings, deep in June,
  When brooding birds stir in the nest,
And heavy dews slip down the leaves,
  And drop into the rose's breast,
I woke and looked into the east,
  And saw no sign of coming day;
The pale cold morning rolled in mist,
  Slept on the hill-tops far away.

My window looked into the dawn,
  The slumbering dawn that was so nigh,
The shadow of the hills was drawn
  In waving lines against the sky.
But warmer hues began to tip
  The edges of the mountain cloud
And morning's rosy cheek and lip
  Glowed softly through her snow-pale shroud.

I turned and gazed into the west,
  The river murmured in my ear
' Gone night, and silence, dreams and rest,
  Another day of toil is here.'

THE ISLE OF SLEEP.

I would I had a fairy boat,
   With every swift bright sail unfurled,
To fly beyond the west, and float
   With night into the under world.

My head sank lower on my arm,
   My eyes re-closed in sleepy bliss,
While fancy wove her subtle charm,
   My dream did shape itself to this:—
Upon a shore whose sands of gold
   Sloped down into a silver sea,
Her radiant pinions all unrolled,
   A fairy boat did wait for me.

And Night with all her splendours pale
   Did walk before me on the deep,
The stars looked through her azure veil,
   And hand in hand with her went Sleep.
Beyond the hills, into the night
   My boat went drifting like the wind,
The stars paled round us, and the light
   Died on our pathway far behind.

And cloudy shapes with rippling hair
   That shaded eyes of dreamy calm,
Formed and dissolved into the air
   Which laved my brow with waves of balm.

THE ISLE OF SLEEP.

Dusk arms upreaching from the sea,
    And shadow-faces, seen and gone,
Toward an isle did beckon me,
    Beyond the farthest gates of dawn.

We drew towards that lonely shore,
    With still and measured motion slow,
I saw the hills lift evermore
    Their massive foreheads crowned with snow,
And underneath, like moonlight fair,
    I saw a hundred fathoms deep,
The crystal columns light as air
    That undergird the Isle of Sleep.

And spire and dome and architrave,
    And pictured window's rainbow gleams
Upshone from out the charmèd wave,
    Afloat upon a sea of dreams.
The sea-moss wove her braided locks
    Along the beach in chains afar,
And lilies smiled among the rocks,
    Peerless and perfect as a star.

A wood of asphodel below
    Uprose as still and sweet as death,
And gliding shapes moved to and fro,—
    I watched them with suspended breath.

Lost loved ones met and clasped me here;
   I looked into their eyes serene,
They spake to me, and I did hear
   As I were walking in a dream.

But even then a wind arose
   That swept the morning mists away,
And showed, unfolding like a rose,
   The bright flower of the perfect day:
And fading—faded like a cloud,
   The hands I clasped, like wreaths of smoke,
While chanticleer crowed shrill and loud,
   And wan and 'wildered I awoke.

THE BATTLE AUTUMN OF 1862.

Under the orchard boughs,
  That drop red leaves like coals into the grass,
    The golden arrows of the sunset fall;
    And on the vine-hung wall
Great purple clusters in delicious drowse,
Beakers of chrysolite and amethyst,
Yet by the sun unkissed,
  Lean down to all the wooing lips that pass,
Brimful of red, red wine
Sweet as brown peasants glean along the castled Rhine.

All sights and sounds are of the Autumn weather;
  The urchin rocking in the trees
    Shakes silver laughter with the apples down,—
  And wading to the knees
    Among the stubble and the husks so brown,
The oxen keeping every patient step together,
Bring in the creaking wain,
High-piled with yellow maize and sheaves of rustling
  grain.

While in the mill, with ceaseless whirr and drone,
With moss and lichens to the roof o'ergrown,
An undertone to every other sound,
The blind old horse goes round.

Gathered along the farm-house eaves
  In noisy congress, see the swallows sit,
Or whirling in mid air like autumn leaves,
  In airy wheels they flit.
Bright rovers of all summer skies,
I follow them with wistful eyes:
To-morrow's sunset they will be
A thousand leagues by land and sea
  Beyond this wintry hemisphere.
Heaven gathers round their joyous wings
The sunlight of perpetual springs,
Soft airs and fragrant blossomings
  Through all the glad round year.

I hear as though I did not hear,
  Along the upland fields remote,
The plough-boy's whistle, silver clear:
  For hark! the herds-man's graver note,
Who hums beneath the orchard boughs,
  The ballad of that grand old man,
  Who marshalled freedom's battle van,
And fell,—no laurel round his brows.

To-day the hero-martyr's grave
   Is shaken by the armèd tread
   Of patriotic soldiers o'er his head,
Not by the footsteps of one slave!

So grows the work that he began,
    Wrought out in slow and toilsome ways,
    Yet ever building through the days,
A grander heritage for man.

Oh! harvest years, foretold so long!
Through seas of blood, through years of wrong,
A people patient brave and strong,
   In camp and field, and battle clang,
'Mid cannon's roar and trumpet's peal,
And shock of war, and clash of steel,
   For you each steadfast blade out-sprang!
In you each loyal heart kept faith
As strong as life, as stern as death;
Though human lives like summer grain
Were sown on every battle-plain;
   Blood of our bravest and our best,
   The red, red wine of life was pressed,
And lost like summer rain.
In dust and smoke of carnage whirled,
   Before those dying eyes still swam
    Those coming years so grand and calm,
The golden Autumns of the world!

Through frost and snow and wintry rains,
　Speed, silent hours!—the Nation waits,
While at her feet the slave in chains,
　Kneels, listening for the coming fates;
And round him droops in soil and dust,
　The bright flag of her stripes and stars:
Speed, Autumn hours!—we wait in trust
No tale of traitor lips can dim,
　Till Liberty's white hand unbars
The broad gates of the glad New Year,*
Unfurls our banner free and clear,
　And ushers Peace and Freedom in!

---

* President Lincoln's Emancipation Proclamation took effect on the first day of the New Year, 1862.

IN WAR TIME.

Into the west the day goes down,
   Smiling and fading into the night;
Is it a cross, or is it a crown
   I have worn through all these hours of light!

Bending over my milk-white curds,
   In my dairy under the beech,
Still the thought of my heart took words,
   And murmured itself in musical speech.

And all my pans of golden cream,
   Set in a silver shining row,
Swam in my eyes like the shimmer and sheen
   Of arms and banners, and martial show.

The bee in his gold laced uniform,
   Drilled the ranks of clover blooms,
And carried my very heart by storm,
   Mocking the roll of the distant drums.

But something choked my singing down,
   Deeper than any song expressed.—

IN WAR TIME.

Is it a cross, or is it a crown
  On my brow invisibly pressed!

Out of the east the star-watch shines,
  Lighting their camp-fires in the gray;
I count their white tents' lengthening lines,
  And think of those who are far away.

Where the yellow globes of the orange grow
  In the southern fields—that slope to the sun,—
Oh say, have my brothers met the foe,—
  Has another Shiloh been lost or won!

For when the moonlight falls across
  The threshold of our cottage door.
My heart is full of a sense of loss,
  As if they would return no more.

Last year when the April days were fair,
  And the harvest fields were ploughed and sown,
Two stalwart boys took each his share,
  But now our father toils alone.

And often at our evening prayers,
  With an absence I can understand,
I see him look at the vacant chairs,
  And wipe his brow with his wrinkled hand.

And therefore at the fireside nook,
    Kneeling sadly at night to pray,
All the light of the holy book
    Seems to fall and point one way.

And therefore tending my milk-white curds,
    Still the song that my fancy hums,
Catches the glitter of martial words,
    And sets itself to the beat of drums.

CHRISTMAS HYMN.

Break over the waiting hill-tops,
   White dawn of the Christmas morn!
For the angels have sung through the midnight,
   That the wonderful Babe is born.

And still in the slumbering valleys,
   The night's black tents are up,
And the young moon stands on the mountains,
   Clear and fair as a silver cup.

Under the cottage rafters,
   Silent and soft and deep,
On the swart low brow of the toiler,
   Settles the dew of sleep.

And some that watch and waken,
   Are dreaming of eyes whose ray
Was long ago quenched and hidden
   Under the shroud away.

Oh, sing thy jubilant anthem
   Over the frozen mould,
And tell that wonderful story
   Again, that never grows old!

For under the year's broad shadow,
  Along the upward way,
Our footsteps often falter,
  And often wander astray.

Weary and weak and erring,
  In sorrow and doubt and tears,
Shine through the mist and the darkness
  Star of a thousand years!

Awhile from the dusty marches
  Of life let us find release,
And pitch our tents in the shadow
  Of the white-walled City of Peace.

Let us hear through the blessed starlight.
  The angels of Bethlehem,
Singing Glory to God in the highest,
  On earth good will to men.

White dawn of the Christmas morning,
  Through the snow-wreaths shining pale,
Let the joy-bells ring through the valleys,
  Hail to thy coming—hail!

TE DEUM LAUDAMUS.

Along the floors of heaven the music rolls,
Fills the vast dome, and lifts our fainting souls:
Praise God! Oh praise Him all created things,
Praise Him, the Lord of lords, the King of kings

Slow pulses coursing darkly underground,
Leap up in leaf and blossom at the sound,
Shake out glad pennons in remotest ways,
And with a thousand voices utter praise.

Along the southern hills the verdure creeps,
And faint green foliage clothes the craggy steeps,
Where in the sunshine lie reposing herds.
Whose gladness has no need of spoken words.

In the deep woods there is a voice, which saith
" The Lord is risen—there shall be no more death!'
Listen, Oh Man! and thy dull ears shall hear
The Easter Anthem of the awakened year.

Past isles of emerald moss the brooklet flows
Melodious, and rejoicing as it goes;

Past drooping ferns, and through the mazy whir
Of insect wings of gold and gossamer.

Praise God!—they whisper softly each to each;
Waves have a voice, and trees and stones a speech;
Day unto day the chant of birds and breeze,
And man alone is dumb, nor hears, nor sees.

A NOVEMBER WOOD-WALK.

Dead leaves are deep in all our forest walks;
  Their brightest tints not all extinguished yet,
  Shine redly glimmering through the dewy wet;
  And whereso'er thy musing foot is set,
The fragrant cool-wort lifts its emerald stalks.

How kindly nature wraps secure and warm,
  In the fallen mantle of her summer pride,
  These lovely tender things that peep and hide,
  Whom unawares thy curious eye hath spied,
For the long night of winter's frost and storm.

Still keeps the deer-berry its vivid green,
  Set in its glowing calyx like a gem;
  While hung above, a marvellous diadem
  Of tawny gold, the bittersweet's gray stem,
Strung with its globes of murky flame is seen.

The foot sinks ankle-deep in velvet moss,
  The shroud of some dead giant of his race;
  Dun gold and green and brown thick interlace,
  Their tiny exquisite leaves in cunning trace,
Weaving their beaded filaments across.

Here mayest thou lie, and looking up, behold
    Far up the stately trees sway to and fro
    In the deep sunny air, with motion slow,
    And whispering to each other weird and low,
The secrets of the haunted cloud-land old.

Heaven seems not half so far as in the town,—
    Looking through smoke and dust and tears to gain
    Some heavenly comfort for thy human pain,
    Heaven seems far off, but here the dews and rain
Come like a benediction from the Father down.

Nor will He who forgets not any weed
    That blooms its little life in forest shade,
And dies when it hath cast its ripened seed,
    Forget the human creatures He has made,
Frail as they are, and full of infinite need.

Now like a sheaf of golden arrows fall
    The last rays of the Indian Summer sun;
    And hark! along the hollow hills they run,
Invisible messengers, the battle-call
Of coming storms, in pipings faint and small
    They bring:—the pageant of the year is done.

RESIGNATION.

If Thou who seest this heart of mine
  To earthly idols prone,
Should'st all those clinging cords untwine,
  And take again Thy own,—
Help me to lay my hands in thine,
  And say Thy will be done!

But Oh, when Thou dost claim the gift
  Which Thou did'st only lend,
And leav'st my life of love bereft,
  And lonely to the end,—
Oh Saviour! be Thyself but left,
  My best beloved Friend!

And still the chastening hand I bless,
  Which doth my steps uphold
Along earth's thorny wilderness,
  Back to the Father's fold,
Where I Thy face in righteousness
  Shall evermore behold.

EUTHANASIA.

> "O Life, O Beyond,
> Thou art strange, thou art sweet!"
> —*Mrs.* Browning.

Dread phantom, with pale finger on thy lips,
Who dost unclose the awful doors for each,
  That ope but once, and are unclosed no more;
  Turn the key gently in the mystic ward,
  And silently unloose the silver cord;
  Lay thy chill seal of silence upon speech,
  And mutely beckon through the soundless door
To endless night, and silence and eclipse.

Even now the soul unfettered may explore
  On its swift wing beyond the gates of morn,
  (Unravelled all the weary round of years)
    And stand, unfenced of time and crowding space,
  With love's fond instinct in that primal place,
  The distant northern isle where she was born;
  She sees the bay, the waves' deep voice she hears,
And babbles of the forms that are no more.

They are the dead, long laid in foreign graves,
  One with his sword upon his loyal breast,

And one in tropic lands beneath the palm ;
  The sea rolls dark between those hemispheres,
  And all the long procession of the years,
Since last those warm young hands she fondly
    pressed,
And heard through mute farewells the funeral
    psalm,
The " nevermore " of the dividing waves.

The record of a life is writ between ;
  The new world's story supplements the old ;
    The heathery hills, the rapture of the morn,
    The fishers' huts, the chieftain's castle gray,
    And the smooth crescent of the land-locked bay,—
  These, the long hunger of the heart outworn,
  New scenes replace, and the once strange and cold,
Become like those kept in the memory green.

But thou hast found already that dread place,
  And thy lost loved ones in that unknown goal,
    Ere thou hast quite put off the scrip and shell,
    And gathered up thy feet into the bed,
    And closed thine eyes, the last prayers being said,
  Thy lips move dumbly, thy delaying soul
    Passes in salutation, not farewell,
To join the heroes of thine ancient race.

J

Unoutlined shadow, angel of release,
  Whose cool hand stills the fever in the veins,
    And all the tumult of life's crowding cares—
      Ambition, envy, love and fear and hate,
      Hope's eager prophecies fulfilled too late,
    And fierce desires, and sorrows, and despairs—
  Thou wav'st thy mystic wand, and there remain
Sleep and forgetfulness, and utter peace.

Why should we fear thy shadow at the door,
  Oh thou mysterious Death?—art thou not sweet
    To the worn pilgrim of life's toilsome day,
      Who com'st at evening time, and show'st instead
      Of pilgrim tent, and pilgrim pallet spread,
    The doors of that vast caravansera
  Where all the pilgrims of the ages meet,
And rest together, and return no more?

BALLAD OF THE MAD LADYE.

The rowan tree grows by the tower foot,
  (*Flotsam and jetsam from over the sea,
  Can the dead feel joy or pain?*)
And the owls in the ivy blink and hoot,
And the sea-waves bubble around its root,
  Where kelp and tangle and sea-shells be,
  When the bat in the dark flies silently.
  (*Hark to the wind and the rain.*)

The ladye sits in the turret alone,
  (*Flotsam and jetsam from over the sea,
  The dead—can they complain?*)
And her long hair down to her knee has grown,
And her hand is cold as a hand of stone,
  And wan as a hand of flesh may be,
  While the bird in the bower sings merrily.
  (*Hark to the wind and the rain.*)

Sadly she leans by her casement side
  (*Flotsam and jetsam from over the sea,
  Can the dead arise again?*)
And watcheth the ebbing and flowing tide,
But her eye is dim, and the sea is wide;

The fisherman's sail and the cloud flies free
And the bird is mute in the rowan tree
  (*Hark to the wind and the rain.*)
The moon shone in on the turret stair
  (*Flotsam and jetsam from over the sea,
    The dead are bound with a chain.*)
And touched her cheek and brightened her hair,
And found naught else in the world so fair,
  So ghostly fair as the mad ladye,
  While the bird in the bower sang lonesomely.
  (*Hark to the wind and the rain.*)

The weary days and the months crept on,
  (*Flotsam and jetsam from over the sea,
    The words of the dead are vain.*)
At last the summer was over and gone,
And still she sat in her turret alone,
  Her white hands clasping about her knee,
  And the bird was mute in the rowan tree.
  (*Hark to the wind and the rain.*)

Wild was the sound of the wind and the sleet,
  (*Flotsam and jetsam from over the sea.
    The dead—do they walk again?*)
Wilder the roar of the surf that beat;
Whose was the form that it bore to her feet
  Swayed with the swell of the unquiet sea,
  While the raven croaked in the rowan tree.
  (*Hark to the wind and the rain.*)

BALLAD OF THE MAD LADYE

Oh Lady, strange is the silent guest—
(*Flotsam and jetsam cast up by the sea,
Can the dead feel sorrow or pain?*)
With the sea-drenched locks and the pulseless breast
And the close-shut lips which thine have pressed
   And the wide sad eyes that heed not thee,
   While the raven croaks in the rowan tree.
(*Hark to the wind and the rain.*)

The tower is dark, and the doors are wide,
(*Flotsam and jetsam cast up by the sea,
The dead are at peace again.*)
Into the harbour the fisher boats ride,
But two went out with the ebbing tide,
   Without sail, without oar, full fast and free,
   And the raven croaks in the rowan tree.
(*Hark to the wind and the rain.*)

THE COMING OF THE KING.

"O thou afflicted, tossed with tempest, and not comforted, behold, I will lay thy stones with fair colours, and lay thy foundations with sapphires. And I will make thy windows of agates, and thy gates of carbuncles, and all thy borders of pleasant stones. And all thy children shall be taught of the Lord; and great shall be the peace of thy children." Isaiah, liv. 11-13.

As the sand of the desert is smitten
   By hoof-beats that strike out a light,
A flash by which dumb things are litten,
   The children of night;
So Thou who of old did'st create us,
   Among the high gods the Most High,
Strike us with Thy brightness, and let us
   Behold Thee, and die.

Grown old in blind anguish and travail,
   Thy world thou mad'st sinless and free
Gropes on, with no power to unravel
   The clue back to Thee:
Since his feet from Thy ways torn and bleeding
   The long march of ages began,
And the gates of Thy sword-guarded Eden
   Were closed upon man.

Fates thicken, and prophecies darken,
  Grown up into blossom and fruit;
And we lean in these last days to hearken
  The sound of Thy foot.
Not now as a star-fallen stranger,
  By shepherds, and pilgrims adored,
As couched among kine in a manger,
  An undeclared lord:

Not now in waste wilderness places,
  And mountains, and wind-shaken seas,
Proclaiming to strange alien races
  The gospel of peace ;
Who rended'st the prey from the leopard,
  With sorrowful wounding and strife,
The Priest—the Lamb slain—the Good Shepherd,
  The way and the life.

Not the face that wept over the city
  Nor that with its anguish of pain
In the garden, unlightened by pity
  Of angels or men ;
Nor the suffering form, unreplying,
  With the chrysm of death at its lips;
Cross-uplifted, and nail-pierced, and dying
  In fateful eclipse :

But with all heaven's glory and splendour
    Through the gates of the morning come down,
And with thrones and dominions to render
    Him sceptre and crown!
With the Face beyond all men's thinking,
    Beholden of all men's eyes;
And the earth in its gladness drinking
    The light of the skies.

With the rapture of angels, the singing
    Of radiant choirs unknown,
And the shouting of glad hosts bringing
    Our King to His throne!
O City of David, the Golden,
    That sittest in darkness so long,
No longer in chains thou art holden,
    Break forth into song!

Arise, and upbuild thy waste places,
    Take helmet and buckler and sword,
And gather from far-scattered races
    The tribes of the Lord!
Thy Prince shall ride onward victorious;
    Full strong are his arrows and fleet;
And high shall His throne be, and glorious
    The place of His feet!

Set thy lips to the trumpet, awaken
  The isles of the South and the North,
As the trees of the forest are shaken
  When whirlwinds go forth :
Like the waves of the sea, like the thunder
  Of armies, with jubilant voice,
A multitude no man can number
  Shall sing and rejoice.

The kingdoms beyond the great river,
  The uttermost isles of the sea,
And peoples and tribes shall deliver
  Thy children to thee.
Once more shall thine ensign, the Lion
  Of Judah, be o'er thee unfurled ;
Once more shall thy gates be, O Zion,
  Set wide to the world !

With hands stretched in mute supplication,
  With longing, and weeping, and prayer,
We have waited for this, thy salvation,
  In grief—not despair ;
Till thy Lord to His temple descended,
  Shall comfort thee, sorrowful one,
And the days of thy mourning be ended,
  Thy triumph begun.

Till the mountains about thee assemble
    Lost lights of the sun-dawn, rose-red,
White splendours, that point as they tremble
    The path for His tread :
Through the hate of our foes, and their scorning,
    And dumb in the darkness we wake,
For the night is far spent—and the morning
    In glory shall break.

WITH A BUNCH OF SPRING FLOWERS.

(In an Album.)

In the spring-time, out of the dew,
   From my garden, sweet friend, I gather,
   A garland of verses, or rather
A poem of blossoms for you.

There are pansies, purple and white,
   That hold in their velvet splendour,
   Sweet thoughts as fragrant and tender,
And rarer than poets can write.

The Iris her pennon unfurls,
   My unspoken message to carry,
   A flower-poem writ by a fairy ;
And Buttercups rounder than pearls.

And Snowdrops starry and sweet,
   Turn toward thee their pale pure faces
   And Crocus, and Cowslips, and Daisies
The song of the spring-time repeat.

So merry and full of cheer,
With the warble of birds overflowing,
The wind through the fresh grass blowing
And the blackbirds whistle so clear.

These songs without words are true,
All sung in the April weather—
Music and blossoms together—
I gather and weave them for you.

THE HIGHER LAW.

Love and Obedience—these the Higher Law
From which Thy worlds have swerved not, singing still
Their primal hymn rejoicing, as at first
The morning stars together. Hast thou heard,
In vast and silent spaces of the sky,
What time the bead-roll of the universe
God calls in heaven, every tiniest star—
From myriad twinkling points—from plummet depths
Of dark too vast for eye and sense to guess,
Send up a little silver answer " I am here."
Even so, the humblest of thy little ones, dear Lord,
May through the darkness hear Thy still small voice,
And answer with quick gladness " Here am I,—
I love Thee,—I obey Thee,—use me too !"

MAY.

Thou comest to the year,
And bringest all things beautiful and sweet;
Thy lovely miracles themselves repeat
    In the green glory of the grass,
And peeping flowers that stay our lingering feet
  With their soft eyes, blue like the sky and clear;
    Thou bringest not, alas,
  Our lily, our May-blossom, O New Year!

Thou bringest all things fair,
And bright, and gentle, but thou bring'st not her:
The May-birds warble, and May breezes stir
    In the sweet-scented lilac boughs;
But our one May—our gentlest minister
  Of gladness, with the beauty of her hair,
    Her place in our still house
  Is empty,—and the world is bleak and bare.

TWO WINDOWS.

I.

One looks into the sun lawn, and the steep
  Curved slopes of hills, set sharp against the sky,
  With tufted woods encinctured, waving high
O'er vales below, where broken shadows sleep.
  Here, looking forth before the first faint cry
  Of mother-bird, fluttering a drowsy wing
Above her brood, awakes the full-voiced choir,
Ere yet the morning tips the hills with fire,
  And turns the drapery of the east to gold,
My wondering eyes the opening heavens behold,
Where far within deep calleth unto deep,
  And the whole world stands hushed and worshipping.
Even thus,—I muse,—shall heaven's gates unfold,
  When earth beholds the coming of her King.

II.

This opens on the sunset, and the sea
  From its high casement : never twice the same
  Grand picture rises in its sea-girt frame
Islets of pearl, and rocks of porphyry

And cliffs of jasper, touched with sunset flame,
And island-trees—that look like Eden's—grow
Palm-like and slender, in gradations fine,
That fade and die along the horizon line,
And the wide heavens become—above—below—
A luminous sea without a boundary.

Nay wistful heart,—at day-dawn, or at noon—
Or midnight watch—the Bridegroom cometh soon;
By yonder shining path—or pearly gate;
The word is sure,—thou therefore, watch and wait.

THE MEETING OF SPIRITS.

From out the dark of death, before the gates
Flung wide, that open into paradise—
More radiant than the white gates of the morn—
A human soul, new-born,
Stood with glad wonder in its luminous eyes;
For all the glory of that blessed place
Flowed thence, and made a halo round the face —
Gentle, and strong with the rapt faith that waits
And faints not: sweet with hallowing pain
The face was, as a sunset after rain,
With a grave tender brightness. Now it turned
From the white splendours where God's glory bur
And the long ranks of quiring cherubim—
Each with wing-shaded eyelids, near the throne,
Who sang—and ceased not—the adoring hymn
Of Holy, Holy! And the cloud of smoke
Went up from the waved censers, with the prayers
Of saints, that wafted outward blessing-freighted ro
Around him standing at the gate alone.
All down the radiant slope of golden stairs,
By which he climbed so late from earth to heaven,
It rolled impalpable—a fragrant cloud;

And still, turned from the Alleluias loud,
Beyond the portal-guarding angels seven,
He listened earthward, for a voice—a sound
Out of the dark that spread beneath profound.

No wind of God stirred in that cloudy land
That bordered all the River's thither side ;
To his that called no voice responsive cried,
Or cleft the dark with flash of answering hand.
And soft the while, sheathed, as it were, within
The noise of heaven's rejoicing, to him stole
Belovèd voices, long to earth a sole
Remembered sweetness only ; sacred kept
As reliquaries are that guard from sin,
And wake the holy aim which else had slept.
How yearned his heart to those long parted ones:
The amaranth, and the sacred flower which grew
A saintly lily by the jasper wall,
Making light shadows on those wondrous stones,
As the wind touched its slender stems and tall,
Turned not to sunward more divinely true,
Than his most worshipping soul to that which made
The light of heaven.

But now the nether shade
Grew luminous with white ascending wings,
And radiant arms of angels, who upbore
With tender hands another soul new-born,

Fairer than that last star whose beaming flings
Another beauty on the brow of morn.
Nearer the lovely vision rose, and more
Aerial clear each moment to his eyes,
Who stood in ecstacy of glad surprise,
And looks of joyous welcome, while the air was stirred
With the swift winnowing plumes approaching.

     This I heard,
And only this,—" Oh ! haste thee, spirit blest,
For thee and me remains at length the rest,
The welcome end of life's long toilsome road,
That leads us to our Father and our God."
And—" Oh beloved, is it thou indeed,
Hast reached before me these fair heavenly lands,
Who taught thine infant lips, with reverent heed
To say Our Father with small upraised hands :
How lovely are thine eyes, that have no pain,
And thy worn cheek, that keeps no travel-stain,
From mid-noon labour called to thy reward ;
While I, at evening, a forgotten sheaf
Still left afield, in mingled trust and grief,
Waited the footsteps of our harvest Lord."

I heard no more—for wave succeeding wave—
A sea of intermittent music swelled and grew,

And filled the dome of heaven, all sharply cut
With spires of glittering crystal: all the land
Throbbed with the pulse of music keen, which clave
A shining path before them : hand in hand—
With their rapt faces toward the throne—the two
Went in together—and the gates were shut.

GEORGE BROWN.

O Leader fallen by the wayside prone,—
O strong great soul gone forth !
For thee the wide inhospitable north,
And east and west, from sea to sea make moan :
    And thy loved land, whose stalwart limbs and brain,
Beneath thy fostering care have thriven and grown
To stately stature, and erect proud head,
    Freedom and Right and Justice to maintain
Here in her place inviolate. Without stain
The name and fame which stood for thee in stead
    Of titles and dominions : all men's praise,
And some men's hate thou had'st, yet all shall weep thee dead ;
O Leader, fallen mid-march in the ways,
Who shall fill up the measure of thy days !

TIDE-WATER.

Through many-winding valleys far inland,
A maze among the convoluted hills,
Of rocks up-piled, and pines on either hand,
And meadows ribbanded with silver rills,
Faint, mingled-up, composite sweetnesses
Of scented grass and clover, and the blue
Wild-violet hid in muffling moss and fern,
Keen and diverse another breath cleaves through,
Familiar as the taste of tears to me,
As on my lips, insistent, I discern
The salt and bitter kisses of the sea.

The tide sets up the river; mimic fleetnesses
Of little wavelets, fretted by the shells
And shingle of the beach, circle and eddy round,
And smooth themselves perpetually : there dwells
A spirit of peace in their low murmuring noise
Subsiding into quiet, as if life were such
A struggle with inexorable bound,
Brief, bright, despairing, never over-lept,
Dying in such wise, with a sighing voice
Breathed out, and after silence absolute.

Faith, eager hope, toil, tears, despair,—so much
The common lot,—together over-swept
Into the pitiless unreturning sea,
The vast immitigable sea.

I walk beside the river, and am mute
Under the burden of its mystery.
The cricket pipes among the meadow grass
His shrill small trumpet, of long summer nights
Sole minstrel: and the lonely heron makes
Voyaging slow toward her reedy nest
A moving shadow among sunset lights
Upon the river's darkening wave, which breaks
Into a thousand circling shapes that pass
Into the one black shadow of the shore.

O tranquil spirit of pervading rest,
Brooding along the valleys with shut wings
That fold all sentient and inanimate things
In their entrenchèd calm for evermore,
Save only the unquiet human soul;
Hear'st thou the far-off sound of waves that roll
In sighing cadence, like a soul in pain,
Hopeless of heaven or peace, beating in vain
The shores implacable for some replies
To the dumb anguish of eternal doubt,
(As I, for the sad thoughts that rise in me):

Feel'st thou upon thy heavy-lidded eyes
The salt and bitter kisses of the sea;
And dost thou draw, like me, a shuddering breath
Among dusk shadows brooding silently?

Ah me, thou hear'st me not: I walk alone.
The doubt within me, and the dark without;
In my sad ears, the waves' recurrent moan,
Sounds like the surges of the sea of death,
Beating for evermore the shores of time
With muttered prophecies, which sorrow saith
Over and over, like a set slow chime
Of funeral bells, tolling remote, forlorn,
Dirge-like the burden—" Man was made to mourn."

FORGOTTEN SONGS.

There is a splendid tropic flower which flings
　Its fiery disc wide open to the core—
　　One pulse of subtlest fragrance—once a life
That rounds a century of blossoming things
　And dies, a flower's apotheosis : nevermore
　　To send up in the sunshine, in sweet strife
With all the winds, a fountain of live flame,
　A wingèd censer in the starlight swung
　　Once only, flinging all its wealth abroad
To the wide deserts without shore or name
　And dying, like a lovely song, once sung
　　By some dead poet, music's wandering ghost,
　Æons ago blown out of life and lost,
　　Remembered only in the heart of God.

TO THE DAUGHTER OF THE AUTHOR OF "VIOLET KEITH."

I never looked upon thy face;
I never saw thy dwelling-place;
My home is by Lake Erie's shore,
Beyond Niagara's distant roar;
And thine where ships at anchor ride,
By fair St. Lawrence's rolling tide,
With half a continent between
Its seas of blue, and isles of green,
And many a mountain's nodding crest,
And many a valley's jewelled breast.
Thou in the east, I in the west;
Yet in this book thou hast to me
An individuality;
Something more tangible and fair
Than any dream or shape of air,
With more than an ideal grace,
And sweeter than a pictured face:
For in this book my thought recalls
The garden quaint, the convent walls,
And thou beneath their shadow set,
A blue-eyed fragrant violet.

So for the maiden of the tale,
Whose brave true heart might break, not fail,
Thyself, my Violet I make,
And love thee for thy mother's sake.

A PRELUDE, AND A BIRD'S SONG.

The poet's song, and the bird's,
    And the waters' that chant as they run
And the waves' that kiss the beach,
    And the wind's—they are but one.
He who may read their words,
And the secret hid in each,
May know the solemn monochords
That breathe in vast still places;
And the voices of myriad races,
    Shy, and far-off from man,
That hide in shadow and sun,
    And are seen but of him who can.
To him the awful face is shown
Swathed in a cloud wind-blown
Of Him, who from His secret throne,
In some void, shadowy, and unknown land
Comes forth to lay His mighty hand
On the sounding organ keys,
    That play deep thunder-marches,
Like the rush and the roar of seas,
    And fill the cavernous arches
Of antique wildernesses hoary,
    With a long-resounding roll,

As they fill man's listening soul
With a shuddering sense of might and glory.

These he shall hear, and more than these
In bird's song, and in poet's scroll;
Something underneath the whole,
A music yet unbreathed—unsung—
Unwritten—incommunicable;
Whispered from no mortal tongue:
What seer nor prophet may rehearse
In oracle, or Delphic fable,
Since the old dead gods were young,
And made with man their dwelling-place;
But he shall hear, of all his race,
The dread wherefore of life and death;
He shall behold the ultimates
Of fears and doubts, and scorns and hates,
And the sure final crown of faith.
And in his ear the rythmic verse
Shall sound the steps of that beyond,
Serene, that hastens not, nor waits,
But holds within its depths profound
The mystery of all lives—all fates—
The secret of the universe.

AN APRIL DAWN.

All night a slow soft rain,
A shadowy stranger from a cloudy land,
Sighing and sobbing, with unsteady hand
    Beat at the lattice, ceased, and beat again,
And fled like some wild startled thing pursued
By demons of the night and solitude,
    Returning ever—wistful—timid—fain—
      The intermittent rain.

    And still the sad hours crept
Within uncounted, the while hopes and fears
Swayed our full hearts, and overflowed in tears
    That fell in silence, as she waked or slept,
Still drawing nearer to that unknown shore
Whence foot of mortal cometh nevermore;
    And still the rain was as a pulse that kept
      Time as the slow hours crept.

    The plummet of the night
Sank through the hollow dark that closed us round,
A lamp lit globe of space; outside, the sound
    Of rain-drops falling from abysmal height
To vast mysterious depths rose faint and far,
Like a dull muffled echo from some star

Swung, like our own, an orb of tears and light
   In the unheeding night.

   But when the April dawn
Touched the closed lattice softly, and a bird,
Too early wakened from its sleep, was stirred,
   And trilled a sudden note broke off, withdrawn,
She heard and woke. All silently she laid
Her gentle hands in our's, with such a look as made
   A rainbow of tears it fell upon,
   Caught from another and a heavenlier dawn,
      Fixed—trembled—and was gone.

www.ingramcontent.com/pod-product-compliance
Lightning Source LLC
Chambersburg PA
CBHW031440160426
43195CB00010BB/802